praise for

protecting my peace

"In *Protecting My Peace*, the reader is taken on a transformative journey of self-care, ancestral might, and self-love. As a tribute to Black women everywhere, this book is a testament to our strength, resilience, and the unparalleled beauty of our journey. This isn't just a book—it's a call to action for Black women everywhere to embrace their authentic selves."

—**Ashley McGirt-Adair**, MSW, LICSW, founder and president of the WA Therapy Fund Foundation, psychotherapist, TEDx international speaker, and author

"Within the pages of *Protecting My Peace: Embracing Inner Beauty and Ancestral Power*, we are prompted to recollect the intricate array of narratives, customs, and insights that Black women have preserved across eras. Beyond a mere manual for self-care, this book displays the splendor of Black womanhood in its entirety."

—**Christen Behzadi**, MD, anesthesiologist and DEI training consultant

"Every page of *Protecting My Peace* resonates with the profound wisdom of our ancestors and the importance of self-care in today's world. A must-read for every woman looking to reconnect with her roots and reclaim her power."

—Dr. Katina Kennedy, DNP, EdD, APRN, FNPc, PMHNP-BC, dual certified family and psychiatric nurse practitioner, author, professor, TV and radio health expert, and entrepreneur

"*Protecting My Peace* is a groundbreaking exploration of Black women's rich heritage, the power of self-care, and the transformative journey to self-love. Through its pages, readers are invited to rekindle their connections to their roots and embrace their radiant selves."

—Shara Ruffin, LCSW, founder of Journey to Licensure, LLC

protecting my peace

protecting my peace

EMBRACING INNER BEAUTY AND ANCESTRAL POWER

ELIZABETH LEIBA

CORAL GABLES

For permission requests, please contact the publisher at:

Mango Publishing Group

2850 S Douglas Road, 2nd Floor

Coral Gables, FL 33134 USA

info@mango.bz

For special orders, quantity sales, course adoptions and corporate sales, please email the publisher at sales@mango.bz. For trade and wholesale sales, please contact Ingram Publisher Services at customer.service@ingramcontent.com or +1.800.509.4887.

Protecting My Peace: Embracing Inner Beauty and Ancestral Power

Library of Congress Cataloging-in-Publication number: 2023945360

ISBN: (pb) 978-1-68481-428-2 (hc) 978-1-68481-429-9 (e) 978-1-68481-430-5

BISAC: HEA012000, HEALTH & FITNESS / Holism

contents

foreword

With deep personal resonance and great pleasure, I introduce *Protecting My Peace* by Elizabeth Leiba. In the following pages, you will embark on a journey that promises to be liberating, moving, and educational for anyone who turns the first page.

Workplace trauma resonates deeply with many, and this book directly addresses our collective experiences in corporate settings. This book explores the impacts of workplace trauma while validating the experiences so many of us have had.

As I delved into the manuscript, I was immediately struck by the depth of knowledge, passion, and truth that Elizabeth Leiba brings to the topic of healing from and moving past trauma. This book is a testament to the lived experiences that many of us have endured but haven't yet learned to navigate.

As a psychological safety consultant, I recognize and spend much time thinking about how workplace trauma shifts our mental health and personal stories. Unfortunately, workplace trauma has been the exchange we have made for a paycheck for over a century. Workplaces worldwide cover their unsafe organizations with phrases like "It's just start-up culture!" or "It's about culture fit!" for too long.

We have been asked to trade giant pieces of ourselves, our happiness, and our lives to be considered worthy of a job, a promotion, a title, or simply respect. Too often, organizations offer mere lip service to addressing workplace trauma instead of implementing actionable change.

This book changes everything.

Elizabeth Leiba challenges and reshapes our understanding and approach to workplace trauma. In a world where microaggressions, racism, and harm in the workplace have become normalized, she is unafraid to speak her truth, share her narrative, and provide a road map for individuals to heal from these toxic environments. Her unflinching address of these issues is vital.

One of the most powerful parts of *Protecting My Peace* is the way in which Leiba effortlessly combines rigorous research with personal narrative. By intertwining her experiences with the broader narrative, she invites us into her world to see how work can shape our experiences and mental health. This book helps to bridge the connection between capitalism, workplace trauma, and their impact on our lived experience. While many of us can relate to the strains workplaces can inflict, there's a path forward highlighted in these pages.

I immensely admire Elizabeth Leiba's ability to distill complex topics and data, making them accessible. This book is a testament to her skill in breaking down intricate concepts, making them understandable for experts and novices.

Whether you are looking to heal from workplace trauma or simply create better workplaces, *Protecting My Peace* promises to engage, educate, and inspire. It is a tribute to the power of Black voices and going after what we deserve in work and life. We all deserve safety, healing, and peace—and not just in our homes.

I invite you to embrace changing the narrative with Elizabeth Leiba. Prepare to be moved, to feel anger, joy, and a whirlwind of emotions.

You deserve a life filled with peace, and this book allows us all to take a collective deep breath and move a step closer to a world where we are empowered to protect our peace.

Madison Butler
Chief Experience Officer
GRAV
August 31, 2023

personal journey and realizations

"Loving oneself isn't hard when you understand who and what 'yourself' is. It has nothing to do with the shape of your face, the size of your eyes, the length of your hair, or the quality of your clothes. It's so beyond all of those things, and it's what gives life to everything about you. Your own self is such a treasure."

—Phylicia Rashad

What does protecting your peace, a state we often struggle to define, look like to you? Most of us have a vague idea of what that looks like. But pinpointing it can be elusive. And we're not sure exactly how to get there. For some, it looks like a blue sky with the sun peeking through a fluffy white cloud. Or like a grassy field of dandelions that we can frolic through and blow fluffy white clouds on green stems to make our dreams come true. For others, it smells like incense, sage, and essential oils. How about lavender or jasmine bubbling gently in a bamboo diffuser? While we wait to enjoy the delectable meal we know will be worth the wait, it smells like our mothers' cooking on a Sunday night, and the first bite is a warm taste of heaven.

Peace feels like seeing an Outlook calendar blank for the day, just like an untouched canvas waiting for us to paint our day. It feels like a warm squeeze from our best friend—a hug that feels as comforting as a fluffy blanket on a cold day. That feeling of safety from the world, even if only for a few moments. We never want it to end and giggle once it does, only to give one more squeeze for the road. It feels like the relief that comes when our ride pulls up to airport arrivals. We sigh and smile because we're home. We are where we belong.

When delving deeper into the notion of peace, we inevitably confront the questions: Do we mean Zen? Rest? A spa day? Relaxation? A massage? But how do we relax when our minds are constantly racing? Yet, despite its enticing imagery, for most of us, peace seems so hard to come by, and if we have it in any measure, we want to protect it at all costs. It's painfully fleeting, so the question arises: How can we truly achieve and maintain it? We don't have time to take stock of what it is, let alone enjoy it. We want to bask in it, but first, we must find it. And there don't ever seem to be enough hours in the day. There's so much to do.

The struggle doesn't stop there. There's so much we want to say, but how do we find the words to express the weariness we feel? Yes, we are tired. We are exhausted. And the fear of telling anyone that we are running on empty is enough to make us ignore that we are pouring from an empty cup. We're giving ourselves to everyone willingly and selflessly. But who is filling us up? How do we replenish what has been depleted, and why can't we identify the source of the tension we constantly feel? We can't explain it, so we ignore that nagging question and "power through" it all. The weight of the world bears down on us, yet we're still expected to keep pushing through.

The burdens become heavier as the days go on. We're tired of fighting. We find ourselves worn out from the relentless demands of life. We shouldn't have to bear it all. We shouldn't have to save the world. We need to take off our capes and save ourselves. Just as flight attendants advise passengers to secure their own oxygen masks before assisting others, we need to prioritize our own well-being first. We must do that before assisting others like small children, the elderly, our neighbors, our coworkers, our siblings, our best friend from high school, our sorority sisters, the people at church, and the homeless family panhandling at the gas station. The list goes on and on. But somehow, we are always the last checkbox, instead of being at the top of the list.

Moreover, the pain of always being last on the list intensifies. As the weight mounts, it becomes clear: We're tired of pretending that we're okay. *We're not okay*. And that's okay. It's natural to feel exhausted when you're constantly faced with situations that make you feel overworked, undervalued, underpaid, and overlooked. This exhaustion is not just physical but also emotional and mental, as the energy we spend justifying our worth can be debilitating. If we know that, then we can figure out how to fix it. You can't fix what you don't name. You can't heal when you don't acknowledge your hurt. You can't grow without stretching yourself to learn that protecting your peace does not have to mean sacrificing yourself. Protecting your peace means prioritizing yourself. And by prioritizing yourself, you can begin to feel whole again and leave behind that nagging feeling that something is wrong that you're afraid to identify or name.

What do I mean by whole again? Many of us have been broken, whether we realize it or not. For many of us, recognizing our struggles is the first step on a healing journey. But there are those among us who have yet to begin this journey of self-awareness and healing.

For those who keep telling us to forget our past, our pain, and the horrors endured by our foremothers, why? We have to name our hurt and pain to understand where the generational trauma is coming from. Only then can we call foul to those who would erase our history from the history books, gaslight us, and tell us to "stop being divisive" and move on. Anyone who has been through trauma knows that part of the healing process is acknowledging and understanding that we are not to blame for our doubts, insecurities, or reactions to this daily assault on our senses. The ultimate gaslight is creating an alternate universe and narrative that forces us to forget the past and believe that it never happened, that if it did, it's irrelevant to our existence today.

Both from anecdotes shared by our parents, mentors, and friends, as well as from our personal experiences, we've learned there's no point in going from pet to threat. These bills have got to get paid, Baby Girl. You already know that. And nobody needs to see those tears. We tell ourselves there's no point in crying because our tears cause resentment. Confusion. Suspicion. Fear! No one will pat us on the back, comfort us, thank us for our vulnerability, or compliment us for our "self-awareness." We'll receive no "kudos" for highlighting the importance of mental health and well-being from coworkers, friends, or strangers.

We've been told we'll be called "emotional." Angry? They'll wonder if we can still do our job effectively. They'll ask if the pressure is "too much" for us. Our tears have always been seen as a weakness and never as a strength. For Black women, unearthing emotions means having to confront what those emotions mean. And that takes time that we don't have. While we balance traditional roles—running our homes and caring for children and parents—we also pursue careers, generate income, and even earn advanced degrees. We're in school part-time to get another degree so we can fight for that raise and promotion we know we deserve. So, taking time to think about our needs, our peace, and our emotions and what they mean is never part of the plan. It never has been in any meaningful way because there isn't enough time in the day.

You wake up and cry in your kitchen before the kids rise for school. Later, as you shower, your tears merge with the stream of water. Hot water. Hot tears. Hot mess. You cry. You cry on the way to work with the radio turned up to drown out the sound of your pain. The bass drops, just like your heart, into the pit of your stomach. Sitting in your car in the parking lot, you suddenly find yourself pounding on the steering wheel, and you're not even sure why. You just know that you have pent-up anger that needs to go somewhere. Anywhere. Tears in the bathroom stall during lunch or rapidly blinking during team meetings on Zoom. You know it's best to turn off your webcam and mute your mic.

Then finally, you sink your weary body into bed at night, knowing the respite will only last a few hours until you have to do this all over again, to infinity. It seems never-ending yet slow, like a car crash you see coming but can't stop—no time to warn or protect yourself from the impending danger ahead. There's nothing you can do, so you sob into your pillow at night, exhausted tears of frustration. Alone in your pain because nobody wants to see a Black woman cry.

This ongoing pain and the sacrifice of our true feelings all come down to one thing: we don't allow our emotions to be seen or heard. Our anger or tears are not acknowledged or examined, even if they're valid. It means our souls cry out, but what they tell us never meets our consciousness, let alone the surface of our existence. Our existence becomes putting one foot in front of the other and pushing forward no matter what. There's no time to stop and think about what that means. There is only time to do what needs to be done: take care of everyone else, pay the bills, climb the corporate ladder, get more education, lobby for promotions, and take care of business. But there is always a cost to doing business. We know that to be true. And there is much to be said about protecting our peace versus the cost of doing it. And who pays that cost? Ultimately, it's us.

As Black women, we often embrace the idea of protecting our peace quietly and alone because it seems to be the easiest way forward. The battles of the world seem insurmountable, and often they are.

Protecting our peace means holding our tongues.

It means silence.

It means not sweating the small stuff. If we start thinking about the small stuff, it may band together with the big stuff and become an army of stuff. The stuff will become a huge snowball we know we can't control as it gathers steam and rolls over everything we've worked so hard to build. And we can't have that. That would be disastrous, right? So, it means putting our heads down and continuing to work harder, even though we know we've already worked hard enough. But we know that no one cares about our tears, is there to wipe them, or wants to see them.

Protecting our peace has come to mean bottling up our emotions so we don't explode. And our emotions are always bubbling just below the surface. We're irritated. We're anxious. We're scared, even though we can't identify one thing that we're scared of. There are just so many, and many we haven't even named, not even to ourselves. But leaving it unnamed makes it even more scary. We don't even ask ourselves what we're afraid of because we fear the answer.

We do know we're afraid of being labeled angry, irritable, and difficult, without knowing that those symptoms often indicate we are in mental distress and our emotional well-being is suffering. But we're told that showing those emotions will harm our success. So, we learn to hold our emotions in check. We go with the flow. We swallow the lump in our throat until it feels scratchy and dry. The tears will well up anyway, only to be blinked back rapidly. We can't let them fall. We won't let them fall. We don't.

Yet, in the face of this emotional struggle, we confront a distressing truth: Nobody seems to care when Black women cry. So, why bother? From a young age, we've learned that our tears go unnoticed. Our own communities have conditioned us to suppress our emotions. The media and the broader world around us cosigned that bill. Then, at work, we learn from our own experiences that it is imperative to suppress any valid emotions—such as anger, frustration, grief, or a sinking, nagging sense of life's overwhelming weight—and stop crying. We're afraid of paying the ultimate cost. Our emotions may repel that very same community that warned us of the danger long ago.

We're not sure exactly when or where we learned that ability. The ability to repress and suppress seems to be coded into our DNA.

We understand inherently that losing control of our emotions means we may miss out on professional opportunities. We've been told since we could understand who we were that grabbing those opportunities is the only way to fulfill our destiny.

We already know we're going to have to work twice as hard. We were told that as well. So why add emotion to an already arduous task? The game is rigged, and it's already going to be harder for us.

Emotions will only take us out of our game. And we don't have time for that if we want to win. So we go into each interaction stoically and unfeeling. Our game face is on. We don't remove it until the game is over. And we don't know when that will be.

To protect ourselves means avoiding friction in our relationships because, as many of us feel, it's our job to nurture and care for everyone and everything. Dealing with our feelings about how overwhelming and burdensome that has become means we may lose control of ourselves. And we're afraid of what that may mean. Where will we put all of these feelings of discomfort, disappointment, and sadness once we unearth them and hold them like soil in our fingers? What will grow once we examine all of that? What does that soil look like underneath all of that? Is it fertile? We suspect it's not soft and warm, but more likely hard and dry, like clay, because that's how we feel inside. But what will we do with that knowledge? What can grow from that? There was a rose that grew out of concrete. But can we do that? We don't know. How can we nurture the earth beneath our feet and make it black and rich like we know it should be?

Protecting our peace has meant not asking any questions. We curtail those feelings, hide those emotions, both good and bad, and don't allow ourselves to cry. So, we hide our tears behind the mask that smiles. We bite our lips to suppress the churning in our belly and the rapid heartbeat that warns us to run. Fight or flight! It's a natural reaction. Our hearts race, our hands shake, and we feel confusion. And later, we will be triggered when we feel danger again. It's a normal response to PTSD. We know that intellectually. But we're talking about our mind and its response to our environment. And our mind is telling us to flee. But we know we must sit still and "be good."

Protecting your peace is not something that's "nice to have." It's mandatory for your survival. Your health, both physical and mental, is your wealth. Actively caring for both aspects can help you conquer life's challenges with ease and resilience—not the promotion, the raise, the degrees, the accolades, the accomplishments, or your title. All of those are nice to have. And we all need to pay our bills. I know we don't live in a utopian world where everything is taken care of. And even if we did, what would the role of Black women be? I can only guess. So, work and responsibilities are a part of all of our lives. However, beyond societal expectations, and amidst all the external obligations, your biggest responsibility remains to yourself. It is impossible to pour from an empty cup, and you deserve peace. You deserve rest. You deserve to take time to think about what makes you happy and to bask in that feeling every day if you need to, and whenever you need to. You deserve all of that and more, Sis. And I promise you that once you start to do that, you'll see what you've been missing, and you'll want more.

Slowing down will speed you up. I know that sounds counterintuitive, but when you give yourself the gift of time, it can make your actions more deliberate and your decisions more thoughtful. This results in overall increased productivity and peace. Taking time for yourself and appreciating yourself teaches you that you are the most important thing. Your body and mind will reward you for that, and then you can go back to conquering the world if you want. But first, think about taking care of yourself. The world won't crumble without your steady hand. Place that hand on your chest and breathe in slowly. Fill your lungs and slowly exhale. Now do it again. Take note of how good that feels, and know that's exactly what you need and deserve. Centering yourself in this moment means you are free to give as much or as little of yourself to others as you wish, but only when you're whole. Remember, saying no is a right; it's a complete sentence that requires no further explanation or justification. So if you don't want to take care of everyone, you don't have to. You never did. It's an impossible task anyway, which sets you up to burn out and hurt yourself in the long run. It's time for you to take care of yourself.

This book is for Black women seeking coping strategies to handle stress, enhance wellness, and heal from unpacked trauma through practices rooted in African tradition. *Protecting My Peace* gives them a glimpse into the healing practices of ancestral care. The ultimate goal is to encourage habits that foster growth and consistency and leverage evidence-based strategies. This results in measurable outcomes for increased well-being.

If you take nothing else away from this book, I want you to take one thing with you that I tell myself almost daily. You are more than worthy, and it's not your fault. It's not your fault if they didn't see your worth. That's their loss! It's not your fault that you're constantly working with little rest and feel chronically exhausted. There's no shame in needing time to rest. In fact, you are courageous in every way for seeking ways to increase your emotional well-being and looking for strategies to increase your peace. Being a Black woman in a world that doesn't feel like it was made for you is not a figment of your imagination. The world as it is has not been designed to nurture and protect you. And knowing that doesn't make you a pessimist or negative; it makes you realistic about what is happening around you. It means that you will need to be your biggest advocate. In the same way you might put others' needs first, it's important to remember to take care of yourself.

In our quest for understanding, this book delves deep, exploring these questions through the lens of the African diaspora and the traditional culture that many of us crave, but that is still elusive. I knew there was so much that was unspoken— from the loving touch of my mother, or the sound of her voice that soothed my angst, to the cerasee tea she brought me when I was ill as a child. But how did I capture the love and wisdom of the foremothers I had never met, but whose love I felt through our shared cultural heritage and experiences? I wanted to explore all of the wisdom and knowledge we already have in our communities, not the pop culture, quick fixes, self-help, and toxic positivity that we see so much of in this social media era.

This book is about transforming how you treat and talk to yourself, about capturing the nurturing from our ancestral roots and the mothers we didn't know, but who were able to overcome insurmountable odds so we could be here today. This book is a thank-you to them and an acknowledgment that their sacrifices were not in vain. This book is a way to keep their love and knowledge alive. This book is an acknowledgment of their love. And we receive it.

We are their legacy. We are them, and they are us. Their blood pulses through our veins. And they would want the best for us. Rest. Peace. Not heartache, hard work, disappointment, or struggle. We are our ancestors' wildest dreams. They wouldn't want us to endure a nightmare of anxiety, stress, and overwork. They would want us to thrive, not just survive. Self-care and treating ourselves with kindness are at the center of that survival, not another degree or burning ourselves out to get that next promotion, no matter what we tell ourselves to the contrary. We have to wake up and rest. Wake up to the idea that true life begins when we put our own happiness and emotional well-being first. It's a must. It's a need, not a want. I want peace for you. You deserve that, and so much more.

If you're ready to embark on this transformative journey of learning to protect your peace, then let's delve further. A part of my practice of healing, focusing on my emotional well-being, and taking time for myself on a daily basis has been incorporating journaling and affirmations to sort through my thoughts. The practice gives me the space to process my emotions in a productive way.

Journaling has transcended mere hobby status to become a cornerstone of modern wellness routines. It's the disciplined practice of recording thoughts, emotions, and experiences, offering a plethora of benefits across the mental, emotional, and creative domains. For Black women, with their unique mental health needs and experiences, this practice resonates even deeper.

In the complexity of the human psyche, self-awareness often emerges as a guiding light. Journaling, in its reflective embrace, cultivates a heightened sense of self-understanding. By giving form to the abstract, writing crystallizes emotions and thoughts, allowing for deeper exploration and insight. In a world awash with distractions, this fosters a return to the inner self, grounding the individual in authenticity and truth.

The therapeutic properties of journaling are well documented,[1] and yet its simplicity should not diminish its significance. The act of putting pen to paper can unleash a torrent of emotion, providing a cathartic release for pent-up feelings. This emotional unburdening creates a space for healing, with the pages

---

1   Smyth, Joshua M., 1998. "Written Emotional Expression: Effect Sizes, Outcome Types, and Moderating Variables." *Journal of Consulting and Clinical Psychology* (66), 1:174–184. doi. org/10.1037/0022-006x.66.1.174.

absorbing pain, frustration, and sorrow, transforming them into a tangible form that can be managed, understood, and ultimately transcended.

Furthermore, journaling forges a pathway to personal development, igniting the conscious pursuit of goals. This written dialogue with oneself serves as both a map and a compass, guiding one toward aspirations while holding one accountable to the chosen path. In the quiet contemplation of written words, there emerges a dialogue with the future self, a negotiation of dreams and desires that aligns purpose with action.

For Black women, the practice of journaling can extend beyond the general benefits, reaching into the heart of unique mental health needs shaped by the intersection of race and gender. The very act of writing becomes a sanctuary, a refuge where experiences of discrimination, marginalization, and societal pressure can be dissected and understood. Here, the pain of the collective becomes personal, and the personal finds voice and validation.

Black women often face unique challenges related to both race and gender. Journaling can be a safe space to process these experiences, articulate feelings, and develop coping strategies. In addition, through journaling, Black women can explore and affirm their cultural identity and heritage. This can foster a sense of empowerment and community connection. Black women may also face disparities in healthcare and wellness. Journaling about health and wellness goals, or even chronicling health symptoms, can be a practical tool for managing and advocating for personal health needs.

By providing a space to reflect on and learn from life's challenges, journaling can contribute to building resilience. This can be particularly important for Black women, who face systemic challenges and inequalities. Journaling can be a solitary activity, but it can also be shared with support groups or therapists. This collaborative approach to journaling can help build a support network tailored to the specific needs and experiences of Black women.

Moreover, the celebration and affirmation of cultural identity find fertile ground within the pages of a journal. Black women can explore, articulate, and embrace their cultural heritage, weaving narratives that honor their roots and resonate with their individual and communal identities. This exploration becomes a dance with history, a poetic affirmation of self that echoes the wisdom of ancestors and the vitality of contemporary existence.

So, journaling is more than a wellness practice; it is a symphony of self, a dialogue with the soul that transcends the mundane and reaches into the essence of being. Its benefits, rich and diverse, find particular resonance with Black women, echoing the unique mental health needs that shape their lives. Journaling becomes a bridge between the internal and external worlds, a sacred space where the personal meets the universal and where the inked page becomes a mirror reflecting the complexities, joys, and sorrows of human existence.

Another dimension of a meaningful wellness practice grounded in emotional self-care is the inclusion of daily affirmations. Affirmations, those deliberate and positive declarations intended to foster a supportive mental environment, transcend mere words to become powerful tools within the wellness landscape. A practice imbued with intentionality and consciousness, affirmations shape thought patterns, cultivate positivity, and align the mind's pursuits with the heart's desires. For Black women, given their unique mental health needs shaped by the interplay of racial and gender dynamics, affirmations assume an especially profound role. They become both a shield and a song, resonating with inner strength and cultural pride.

In the pursuit of wellness, affirmations function as architects of thought, molding the mental terrain to create landscapes imbued with positivity, resilience, and self-belief. Through repeated declarations, the mind learns to replace negative, self-limiting beliefs with constructive, empowering truths. It's akin to planting seeds in a garden of consciousness, where, with nurturing care, they grow to become blooming thoughts that enrich life's experience.

The resonance of affirmations with mental well-being lies in their intrinsic connection with the self's narrative. They are a conversation with the innermost self, a dialogue with aspirations, fears, and hopes. This conversation transcends the superficial to delve into self-identity, fostering a relationship with the self that's rooted in acceptance, compassion, and understanding. In the reflection of these positive words, the individual finds not just solace, but empowerment.

Affirmations are also gateways to mindfulness, anchoring the individual in the present moment. They act as reminders of the present's intrinsic value, drawing attention away from past regrets and future anxieties to the here and now. In this sacred moment, affirmations become a meditative practice, harmonizing mind and body in a symphony of present awareness.

The practice of affirmations finds a particularly poignant voice among Black women, given the multifaceted challenges they often face. Society's stereotyping, discrimination, and gender bias create a unique mental battleground that demands resilience, strength, and self-assurance. Affirmations become a nurturing voice in this environment, echoing with affirmations of beauty, wisdom, and strength that resonate with the richness of Black culture and identity.

These affirmations, carefully chosen and lovingly repeated, act as balm for the scars left by societal injustices. They remind Black women of their inherent worth, their unbreakable connection with a vibrant cultural heritage, and their right to happiness and fulfillment. In a world that may sometimes overlook or undervalue their unique experiences, affirmations become a self-affirming declaration of existence, worth, and empowerment.

The communal aspect of affirmations, shared among Black women in support groups or circles of friends, weaves a fabric of collective strength and understanding. These shared words resonate with common experiences, joys, and struggles, creating bonds that transcend individuality and embrace community.

Affirmations as a wellness practice are not mere utterances, but a rich tapestry of intentional positivity, self-awareness, empowerment, and healing. For Black women, they are a poetic dance with the self, resonating with the unique mental health needs sculpted by their individual and collective experiences. In the echo of these powerful words, there's a melody of resilience, a song of self-love, and a chant that speaks of a timeless connection with a vibrant and unbreakable cultural legacy.

journaling questions

1. How would you personally define peace, self-care, and emotional well-being in your life? How do these definitions align with or differ from societal or community perspectives?

2. What strategies or methods are you currently employing to take care of your mental health? How effective have these been in promoting your overall well-being?

3. Have you engaged with traditional mental healthcare practices? If so, what has your experience been like? What differences or similarities have you found between these methods and your personal or community-based approaches to mental health?

4. Are there any ancestral or cultural methods of emotional well-being that you practice or feel connected to? How do these methods contribute to your understanding and practice of peace and self-care?

5. Have you ever utilized journaling or affirmations as a form of self-care? How have these practices impacted your emotional well-being?

6. What challenges or barriers have you faced in your journey toward achieving peace and emotional well-being? How have you addressed or overcome these challenges?

7. How do your family, friends, and community support or influence your practices of self-care and mental health? What role do these relationships play in your overall emotional well-being?

8. What goals do you have for your emotional well-being and self-care practices? How are you planning to achieve these goals, and what resources might you need?

9. How would you describe the conversation around mental health and self-care within the community of Black women? What unique experiences or perspectives do you feel you bring to this conversation?

10. How do you see the intersection of your identity as a Black woman with your self-care and mental health practices? Do you feel that there are unique aspects of your experience that require specialized understanding or support in the mental health field?

affirmations

1. I am worthy of peace and tranquility: My inner peace is a reflection of my strength, and I prioritize nurturing it every day.

2. My self-care is a necessary priority: I embrace taking care of myself, knowing that self-care is not selfish but essential for my mental and emotional well-being.

3. I am resilient and strong: My heritage and personal journey have shaped me into a resilient woman, capable of overcoming challenges with grace and wisdom.

4. I am in control of my emotions: My feelings are valid, and I honor them by allowing myself to feel and then moving forward, guided by my inner wisdom.

5. My mental health matters: I am committed to seeking support when I need it and taking the steps necessary to nurture my mental well-being.

6. I honor my ancestors through my self-love: I recognize the wisdom and strength in my lineage and honor it by loving and taking care of myself.

7. I am enough, just as I am: My value is inherent, and I don't need to prove myself to anyone. I am enough in my authenticity.

8. I surround myself with love and positivity: I consciously choose the people and environments that uplift me, recognizing that I deserve love, respect, and kindness.

9. I am an agent of change and growth in my life: I have the power to make positive changes in my life and strive continually toward personal growth and fulfillment.

10. I embrace my unique journey with gratitude: I recognize the beauty and uniqueness of my path as a Black woman, and I navigate it with courage, love, and gratitude.

chapter 2

the plight of Black women

"Black women are the mules of the world."

—Zora Neale Hurston

In addition to my own experience with the challenge of not only prioritizing my own physical and mental health, but also finding the courage and tools to do so, I've spent more than twenty years working in higher education as a counselor, faculty member, and director in the c-suite of my organization for a decade. I typically worked with a variety of students: those in career colleges, community colleges, and others who were still exploring their paths. I felt they would benefit most from seeing and feeling my presence in the classroom. I wanted to give them everything I had never received during my undergraduate years—encouragement, mentorship, nurturing, and listening. My primary goal was always to help my students see that they were more than their present circumstances and surroundings. Many were first-generation students, immigrants to South Florida, single parents, or working adults; some had been incarcerated; and most had overcome insurmountable odds. But I approached each one with no judgment—only a deep desire to see them reach their maximum potential.

When I started writing *I'm Not Yelling*, my goal was to take the knowledge I had gained from advocating for Black folk, and especially Black women, to be empowered in every space they inhabited, and to leverage their voices to step into their true calling. I had expanded my classroom beyond a physical building and taken to social media and mainstream media to share my love and support for Black women. But it wasn't until I started to do research for the book that I was confronted with the troubling statistics from study after study. Black women were suffering from a myriad of physical and mental health ailments from racial trauma, microaggressions, and feelings of Imposter Syndrome, or what I had identified as Imposter *Treatment*, from being constantly under assault in the predominantly white environments of corporate America. We were tired and feeling undervalued, and we knew we weren't being appreciated.

Many, if not all, of the women I spoke with, as well as the experts I consulted, confirmed that they were all searching for something more in their lives. We needed to heal from all of this trauma. We were looking for strategies to manage our stress and discontent. And, even worse, we were scared to even voice the turmoil we were feeling inside. So, just as I had done with *I'm Not Yelling*, I set out on a journey to find answers. Why were Black women feeling so overwhelmed? Why did we all share this feeling of exhaustion, and what were the sources? What could we do to find joy, healing, peace, and contentment? And what could we do beyond therapy and medical interventions? What were some of the ways we could learn to consistently prioritize ourselves and make that a habit until we naturally gave ourselves what we so desperately needed? I wanted to provide context for our feelings. You are not imagining this, Sis!

Those feelings of exhaustion are real and valid. You deserve rest, and I wanted to explore what that would look like. Not just collapsing into bed at the end of the work day, only to wake up tired and do it all over again. How could we find rest in our everyday existence and hold onto that? That was the reason for writing *Protecting My Peace*. I wanted to find out how to do it for myself, and I wanted to share what I found out with the Black women I love. I call *I'm Not Yelling* my love letter to Black women, and *Protecting My Peace* is a continuation of the same. We deserve love, peace, and happiness every day, and I wanted to show how much better life can be when those things are first on our to-do list. We are the first item at the top of that list. What does prioritizing ourselves on our to-do list look like? How does that feel?

For me, the journey to healing began when I finally took the first step to acknowledge my pain. I sank to the worst depths of despair I could ever imagine. It was then that I realized something had to change. So, one afternoon in the middle of the week, I packed one duffle bag with only my clothes and fled my home state to escape a cycle of physical, emotional, and financial domestic abuse that had lasted more than a decade. I didn't know what faced me ahead, but I knew nothing could be worse than everything I had already endured. My job, marriage, family, and relationships were shredded at the seams from my exhaustion and lack of focus on putting myself first. I didn't even know how to attend to my own needs, because I never had. But now I had no choice. If I didn't commit to taking care of myself, the consequences would be disastrous for my health and even my life.

The diagnosis of severe anxiety and post-traumatic stress disorder initially shocked my body. My heart pounded uncontrollably, my hands were constantly shaking, and I couldn't get my mind to stop racing to slow my thoughts down even momentarily. Work and life seemed impossible to balance, so I knew my best option was therapy and consulting with a psychiatrist to explore more deeply what was happening to my mind and body. I had been resistant to that idea for almost a year. I didn't want to admit I didn't "have it together." I was ashamed of what I had endured, unable to articulate why I had let it go on or acknowledge how damaging it had been to my soul and my very existence in the world. I felt like there must be a way for me to overcome this. I looked at what I had been able to do. I had walked through the fire, and even though I'd been burned, I had survived. But even though I had survived, I struggled to make it through each day. I prayed for night to come so I could close my eyes. There were times when I wished I would never wake up. I had hit a wall, and I didn't know how to "push through" anymore. I wanted help. I needed help.

Finding a Black woman in the mental health field—one I could trust—became its own challenge. I almost gave up. But as each spiral got worse and worse, I knew this had to be faced, and I needed to talk to someone who looked like me. No judgment. No blame. Just the freedom to speak my truth and find comfort in knowing that, not only was I normal, but everything was going to be okay.

Eventually, I found a Black woman psychiatrist who was seventy years old—the same age as my mom. And at the end of our first session, she told me to give myself a big hug. She congratulated me for overcoming fear and taking the first step to take care of myself and what she called the chemicals in my brain. Not that I was sick. Not that I was bad. Not that I was a disappointment. I had chemicals in my brain that needed to be managed so I could feel better and heal.

I received confirmation of the anxiety and PTSD I suspected I was suffering from as a result of more than a decade of unaddressed trauma. In addition, I found out I was also struggling with the symptoms of both bipolar disorder and attention deficit disorder (ADHD). Initially, I cried—a mixture of relief, sadness, and fear. I felt like the bottom of my world had fallen out from underneath me. But it explained so much about what I was going through in the present, and how I had handled most of my life. I often couldn't think clearly or concentrate, even though I was an "A" student as an undergrad at a top university and had earned three master's degrees in business, organizational management, and interdisciplinary studies with a focus in English and writing. I was also a college professor for more than a decade.

But, for reasons I couldn't articulate during that time, I had largely not been happy. And when I did feel joy, it was fleeting and hard to recapture. I had always felt like there was something more that would relieve this feeling of emptiness. With each degree, accomplishment, promotion, and milestone like marriage and children, the emptiness only subsided temporarily, then came back with a vengeance, as if to let me know it would not go quietly. I knew that the peace I sought wouldn't be found in any of those things. It was inside me, and I needed to take my doctor's advice. I needed to take care of myself. I needed to love myself with everything I had inside. I needed to hug myself and not let go.

With this newfound knowledge of my diagnoses and understanding of my mental and physical states, I pondered how I could apply it to my healing journey. What did it mean for me regarding how I would function for the rest of my life? I was bold. I was outspoken. I was Black excellence. I was Black Girl Magic personified. I was all the things. All of them. I was unstoppable. I was more than a conqueror. But when I looked in the mirror and touched my face, I looked sad. I looked tired. I was. I looked afraid. I was. This Black woman had been running on empty for so long that she didn't remember ever resting.

I couldn't remember when I had last been happy. I was chronically tired and uninterested in most things, including my job and even my friendships. And I was in pain both physically and mentally. Recognizing that my past attempts at seeking therapy during times of stress were not enough, I committed to ongoing therapy as a crucial step on my healing journey.

Stressed. That word seemed so inadequate to describe what I was going through, not only currently, but also in the past. It was laughable that I had shrugged off these feelings of always being overwhelmed, like I was wading in mud, and always running without resting as normal. I would need to determine a new normal in order to change my lifestyle and decrease my stress level. As I committed to getting better, I wanted to think about my journey holistically, to match the way I approach everything in my life. I'm a researcher and problem solver by nature, so I decided to think about not only my own healing journey, but also that of all of the other Black women I had met since writing my first book, *I'm Not Yelling: A Black Woman's Guide to Navigating the Workplace*.

After speaking with dozens of women I met across social media, at book signings, during panel discussions, and during interviews on my podcast on EBONY Media, I concluded that I was not alone in my challenge to balance my mental health and emotional well-being. And I was also not alone in feeling a deep and desperate urge to heal my exhausted body and soul fully. After more than twenty years working in nonprofit, sales, media, and higher education, I could count the raises and promotions I had received on one hand. And each one I'd had to fight for. I'd had to justify myself. I'd done everything to prove myself, including working myself to exhaustion. I had never taken a vacation from work. Ever.

In addition to my mental health diagnosis, I had received an epilepsy diagnosis of unknown causes a few years prior. My body had undergone surgery for uterine fibroids. I had endured two high-risk pregnancies. I wanted to understand why. Why were Black women so prone to these physical and mental health ailments? What was the root cause that left us so depleted in every way? What strategies or remedies could I add to my wellness practice besides the therapy and medication I had already committed to? And how could I incorporate practices that built on the knowledge I gained while writing my bestselling book, *I'm Not Yelling*?

Black women's experiences are unique to our circumstances and how we navigate the world. I knew that based on the research I had already done. In talking to Black women, I learned that many were looking for coping strategies for stress, wellness, and emotional well-being, as well as healing unpacked trauma. They were challenged with articulating their stressors and wanting to accurately determine the source of these stressors. They sought holistic solutions that focused on their minds, bodies, and souls—to reveal the entirety of their beings in all of their glory. Each of the women I spoke to was ready to unfurl her wings and soar like a phoenix, rising from the ashes of the past and kissing the sun to greet a new day—the beginning of a brand-new existence.

Another important fact I learned during research for *I'm Not Yelling* was that the unique history and culture of Black folk, and particularly Black women, have been the foundation that has strengthened, comforted, and guided us through unspeakable obstacles, trials, and stumbling blocks. Yet, through it all, we are still here. We are still standing. Despite the pain, we have found a way to push through. And I wanted to understand how. Despite a unilateral war that was waged physically, mentally, and spiritually across the African diaspora, we managed to walk through fire and survive. The fires that burned in Rosewood, Tulsa, and Seneca Village were not conjured up like hoodoo, a part of a collective tall tale, or just a figment of our vivid imaginations.

So, how do we tap into the traditions that have allowed our communities to continue to survive, even after all of the turmoil and trauma we have endured? What can we do to honor our ancestral roots, which signify the resilience and tenacity inherent in our heritage? Pan-African activist, journalist, and entrepreneur Marcus Garvey was a strong advocate for understanding and celebrating our roots. He famously wrote, "A people without knowledge of their past history, origin, and culture is like a tree without roots. Trees that are not firmly rooted in rich, fertile soil do not grow, do not bear fruit, they cannot withstand strong wind, or bear heavy loads."[2] Our ancestors blazed a path of joy, resilience, and strength for us to follow, and they did so with intention. None of it was accidental. I really wanted to understand how that could possibly be. We turned our stumbling blocks into stepping stones. How did we do it collectively in the past? And how could we harness that knowledge today to improve our mental, spiritual, and emotional well-being?

Some of us may only have a vague understanding or awareness of ancestral knowledge and spirit. But for many of us, delving into this knowledge in search of answers seems like an overwhelmingly daunting task. Perhaps we have been taught that knowledge is not applicable to our modern-day lives. I'd counter that it is more beneficial now than ever before. Maybe we think there is something wrong with seeking this type of knowledge because it runs counter to our upbringing or religious beliefs. My response to anyone, and even myself, is that this type of knowledge predates anything we currently know because it is integral to our very identity and coded into our DNA, running through our veins in a way that nothing else can. It is literally a part of us, and the emptiness and yearning we feel often can't be reconciled until we find that missing puzzle piece to make ourselves complete.

Some may believe that leaning on this awareness may be harmful or cause others to judge them or their intent. We have all seen the memes and jokes about "Hotepry," a term often used to mock pseudo-intellectualism, on social media. It seems as though everything is designed to pull us away from ancestral ties that have bound our communities and sustained them for hundreds of years here in America, and for hundreds of thousands of years prior in African antiquity. What if we ran toward our ancestral ties and traditions instead of running away

2   Gray, Sara. 2021, "Deeply Rooted in Black History—National Equity Project." National Equity Project. www.nationalequityproject.org/blog/black-historys-deep-roots.

from them, as we were taught to do? What if we could decolonize our minds and incorporate the nourishment from traditional practices that have been our legacy since the dawn of civilization? What if we chose to run into the loving arms of the people who knew us before we knew ourselves, sacrificed so much so we could be here, and left a legacy for us to follow? What might that mean for us, not only individually but also collectively?

So, with all of that in mind, I made a conscious decision to uncover gems, gold, and hidden treasure. I knew it was waiting for me to discover it. But I sought this knowledge not for exploitation, unlike the colonists, who stole cultural treasures for their own selfish endeavors. I wanted something more beyond the clinical questionnaires, pharmaceutical drugs, and countless hours of therapy learning coping skills and strategies to overcome the racing thoughts and sinking feelings I was experiencing daily. Recognizing my own struggles, I understood how desperately I needed those interventions. But my ancestors didn't have any of those tools, strategies, or resources. So, what did they do to encourage themselves, to center themselves, to love themselves, to heal themselves fully, and to keep going for me? I needed to know.

The complex web of challenges we face as Black women is not just personal—it's also deeply historical. This is captured in the concept of post-traumatic slave syndrome (PTSS), as explained by renowned author, academic, and researcher Dr. Joy Angela DeGruy, which explains the etiology of many of the adaptive survival behaviors in African American communities throughout the United States and the diaspora. It is a condition that exists as a consequence of the multigenerational oppression of Africans and their descendants resulting from centuries of chattel slavery. This form of slavery was predicated on the belief that African Americans were inherently or genetically inferior to whites. Institutionalized racism came after this and continues to cause harm. Under such circumstances, these are some of the predictable patterns of behavior that tend to occur: vacant esteem; marked propensity for anger and violence; racist socialization and internalized racism.[3]

To not acknowledge the mental trauma that we, the children of stolen and sold Africans, have endured intergenerationally is to participate in the same dismissive attitude of those in the majority, who constantly tell us through narratives seen in the news media, television, film, and even in the school system that any lack of resilience or motivation has absolutely nothing to do with the hundreds of years of trauma and horror we have endured. The subtext here is, "Just work harder." This results in higher levels of stress and anxiety regarding a goal you suspect is unattainable. And the cycle continues as you race toward each goal you think is the finish line, only to have the goal marker move farther beyond you yet again.

This situation brews a mental and emotional storm, depriving us of the essential rest and well-being we need to function effectively. Many of us fail to acknowledge just how depleted we are without this fundamental care. Historically, acknowledging this depletion has often been stigmatized. A lack of resources and understanding of the benefits has made mental health care seem like a luxury. This is a luxury that most in our community cannot afford. Financially and emotionally, the price seems much too high. The reality we face is to grit our teeth and bear through each challenge, despite most of us lacking the knowledge, models, or coping skills to surmount the numerous obstacles flung into our path. And even if we seek wise counsel, those older mentors and elders have not encountered the more recent evolutions of racism that were not prevalent during their own interactions with those in the majority.

So each generation wades into uncharted waters, our days full of anxiety as we navigate systems that were not designed for us, or people who don't look like us

---

3   "Post Traumatic Slave Syndrome," n.d., Dr. Joy DeGruy. Accessed June 26, 2023. www.joydegruy. com/post-traumatic-slave-syndrome.

but insist that the only way for us to be successful is to assimilate to being more like them, which we know intellectually as well as spiritually to be impossible. We bring a unique energy and perspective, one that often doesn't align with the mainstream view. Regardless of our efforts, it's impossible to repress our authentic selves to match these expectations. And society at large is well aware of that, even if not fully consciously. That leaves them free to interpret our actions in any way they desire, and absolutely not in the empathetic language framed by understanding the ramifications of post-traumatic slave syndrome. With that lens, they would need to examine their own actions in the past, present, and future. They refuse to do that in any meaningful or measurable way.

They would rather blame poor parenting, poverty (without acknowledging how their systems are to blame), and a general lack of motivation for these issues. There is no interrogation of a system purposely designed to subjugate Black people, first to the level of animals that were less than human, then as perfectly equal humans "asking" (or begging) simply for the autonomy to fully participate in society and make our own choices on a 150-year journey to prove our humanity to the very people who told us we were subhuman. The hypocritical gaslighting of such a foolhardy quest, and how emotionally harmful it is to embark on it every single waking day of our lives, is somehow lost in our desire to prove them wrong and even to validate ourselves, while their desire is to maintain that status quo that leaves us constantly questioning every step we take and constantly calculating the risk versus reward of each step, living in a state of hypervigilance that can only clinically be described as PTSD, or more accurately, the post-traumatic slave syndrome explained by Dr. DeGruy.

In 1961, author James Baldwin was asked by a radio host about being Black in America. He said:

> To be a Negro in this country and to be relatively conscious is to be in a state of rage almost all of the time—and in one's work. And part of the rage is this: It isn't only what is happening to you. But it's what's happening all around

you and all of the time in the face of the most extraordinary and criminal indifference—the indifference of most white people in this country—and their ignorance.

Now, since this is so, it's a great temptation to simplify the issues under the illusion that if you simplify them enough, people will recognize them. I think this illusion is very dangerous because, in fact, it isn't the way it works. A complex thing can't be made simple. You simply have to try to deal with it in all its complexity and hope to get that complexity across.[4]

Living life in that manner can never be healthy, no matter what anyone says to the contrary. The experience of constantly navigating indifference leaves those of us in the Black community seeking a sense of closure we know may never come. Just as in an abusive relationship, you seek validation from the very person who is hurting you and experience extreme isolation, exhaustion, and anger. The complexity of a puzzle that seems as though it should be solvable, but has infuriatingly been posed as a low-stakes game of your own making, also creates a sense of hopelessness, where your concerns are dismissed even though the weight of them is literally crushing you alive. The resulting impact has huge mental health implications that have continued to plague our community generation after generation and manifest in the anxiety, depression, and feelings of hopelessness that many in our Black communities feel, particularly the matriarchs of most communities—Black women.

There are, however, those working tirelessly to address these issues. One such individual is Tamika Lewis, the Founder and CEO of WOC Therapy, Inc. Her organization takes a trauma-informed, culturally competent approach to working with clients. Her practitioners teach clients how to reprogram painful past learning by getting to the source of limiting thoughts and beliefs. They also

---

4   Baldwin, James. 2020. " 'To Be In A Rage, Almost All The Time': 1A." NPR. www.npr. org/2020/06/01/867153918/-to-be-in-a-rage-almost-all-the-time.

encourage clients to ask more generative questions, such as "What happened to me?" instead of "What's wrong with me?" In addition, her practice explores historical and institutional racism and its impact on mental health in BIPOC communities. As a master's-level trained social worker and mental health expert, she draws from over fifteen years of experience working with agencies such as UCLA Medical Center, DCFS, and Children's Hospital of Los Angeles, with an extensive background in educational counseling specializing in working with teens and women.

In her 2021 article on Black women and depression, she discusses the significant health issues faced in the US. One of the most prevalent of these issues is mental illness. This is especially true within the African American population, where major depressive disorder (MDD) is particularly common. Though there has been an increase in awareness, there are still major hurdles we need to face.

In a recent large-scale national survey, a lifetime prevalence rate of 10.4 percent was reported for depression among African Americans.[5] This suggests that depression affects African Americans at a high rate. The data also showed that African Americans are more likely to have feelings of sadness, worthlessness, and hopelessness than white Americans. That's well over four million Americans who are faced with psychiatric symptoms and conditions.

It is well-known that unfair laws, policies, and practices have had a significant negative impact on African Americans for the entire history of the United States. Though times have changed, African Americans are still suffering from these laws and policies. There are still a lot of aspects of the Black experience that are damaging, both mentally and physically. No one understands this more than the average African American woman. They are among the most discriminated-against groups in the US, and are often forced to handle and navigate harsh

5   Ward, Earlise C., Jacqueline Wiltshire, Michelle A. Detry, and Roger L. Brown, 2013. "African American Men and Women's Attitude Toward Mental Illness, Perceptions Of Stigma, And Preferred Coping Behaviors." *Nursing Research* (62), 3:185–194. doi.org/10.1097/nnr.0b013e31827bf533.

and hostile situations and environments. Racism, sexism, colorism, and even xenophobia are all causes of stress and MDD, and this has been the truth for centuries.

What's most alarming about MDD among historically excluded communities is the lack of support and resources. Due to the stigma surrounding psychiatric disorders, many African American women don't actively seek treatment for symptoms. Instead of therapy, self-care, or antidepressants, they turn to poor coping habits and mechanisms. There is also a huge lack of representation within the field of study for mental well-being, so it's much harder to connect to therapists and doctors, or to even find WOC therapists.

As mentioned before, African Americans have problems when it comes to seeking help for MDD or any similar condition. African American depression statistics from the CDC reported that African American women are 4 percent more likely to have symptoms of MDD than whites, and are less likely to report it or seek treatment. One of the major problems is a lack of representation; because there are few African American counselors, it's hard for African American women to build trust in therapy care. Another issue is the mistrust of antidepressants and similar medications.

Post-traumatic stress disorder (PTSD) and MDD are both serious mental health conditions, but they differ significantly in their causes and symptoms. MDD is a condition characterized by overwhelming feelings of sadness, hopelessness, and worthlessness, which can affect your daily life in many ways. It can cause insomnia, memory loss, unhealthy weight loss, an increase in heart problems, a weakened immune system, dietary issues, and so on. It can happen to anyone, and episodes can strike at any moment without warning.

PTSD is a condition that develops from a traumatic experience, and can cause chronic pain and fatigue, panic attacks, social isolation, heart disease, social anxiety, eating disorders, and many other effects. In contrast to MDD, PTSD episodes can still occur at any time when a memory or feeling of a traumatic event or experience triggers them.

Due to the harsh reality that women of color face on a day-to-day basis, having MDD and PTSD is far more likely for them than for their male counterparts. Yet Black women's mental health remains a widely ignored issue.[6]

During my time hosting the Black Power Moves podcast on the EBONY Covering Black America Podcast network, I met and interviewed several psychiatrists and psychologists to learn more about the unique mental health challenges faced in the Black community. There are multiple compounding issues that lead to a lack of awareness and care, which include the stigma of mental health illness, a lack of access to resources, and the difficulty of finding therapists who look like us, let alone have cultural awareness of racial trauma and its effects.

In the next chapter, we'll delve further into some of these challenges, and how to consistently practice self-care in a way that helps us embrace ancestral knowledge in combination with evidence-based traditional strategies.

6   Lewis, Tamika. 2021. "Black Women and Depression." WOC Therapy. woctherapy.com/black-women-and-depression.

journaling questions

1. How have you worked to prioritize yourself in your daily life, and what challenges have you encountered? How do you balance the needs of others with your own needs for self-care and healing?

2. Can you describe your personal journey to healing and self-discovery? What have been some pivotal moments, lessons learned, or obstacles overcome along the way?

3. How do you recognize when you need rest, and how do you honor that need? How does rest fit into your overall perspective on self-care and well-being?

4. In what ways have you explored or integrated ancestral knowledge into your self-care practices? How has tapping into this wisdom influenced your approach to healing?

5. How do you recognize and address racial trauma in your life? What supports or resources have been essential in acknowledging and healing from these experiences?

6. How have you come to understand the importance of mental health care in your life? What actions have you taken to ensure that your mental health needs are being met?

7. How does your community influence or support your healing journey? What role do relationships play in your overall wellness and your ability to prioritize yourself?

8. How do you view personal growth and transformation in the context of healing and self-care? What practices or strategies have been particularly transformative for you?

9. How do you see the intersection of your identity as a Black woman impacting your mental health and self-care needs? How do you navigate the unique complexities this intersectionality may present?

10. How do you approach wellness in a holistic way, considering not only mental health but also physical, spiritual, and emotional aspects? How does this approach contribute to your overall sense of well-being and your journey toward healing?

affirmations

1. I value and prioritize myself, recognizing that my well-being is essential. I am worthy of time, care, and attention.

2. I am committed to my healing journey, embracing each step with courage and openness. I grow stronger and more self-aware every day.

3. I honor my body's need for rest, understanding that it is not a sign of weakness but a vital part of my self-care and rejuvenation.

4. I connect with the wisdom of my ancestors, allowing their strength and insight to guide my self-care and healing practices.

5. I acknowledge the racial trauma I have experienced, and I am empowered to heal. My experiences shape me, but they do not define me.

6. I recognize the importance of mental health care and take proactive steps to nourish my mental well-being. I seek support when needed, knowing it's a sign of strength.

7. I embrace the support of my community, knowing that connection and mutual care enhance my journey to well-being.

8. I celebrate my growth and transformation, knowing that each step forward is a victory on my path to healing and self-discovery.

9. I honor the unique aspects of my identity as a Black woman, recognizing that my self-care must be responsive to my specific experiences and needs.

10. I approach my well-being holistically, nurturing my mental, physical, spiritual, and emotional health. Each aspect is vital to my overall wellness and joy.

chapter 3

the prevalence of mental illness in the Black community

"Mental Health is our 'silent' crisis. There is no shame in speaking out and seeking help."

—Viola Davis

In the shadowy recesses of our society, where oppression and inequality often reside, lies an issue of profound significance—the prevalence of mental health disorders in Black women. This issue, neither whispered nor silent, but rather a cry that echoes through generations, speaks to the injustices experienced by an oft-marginalized community that resides in the intersectionality between race and gender. Specifically, major depressive disorder (MDD) and post-traumatic stress disorder (PTSD) serve as haunting refrains within this narrative.

Major depressive disorder, a dark fog that settles on the soul, manifests with particular intensity in Black women. Research demonstrates that they experience this disorder at a rate 50 percent higher than their white female counterparts.[7] Here, MDD is not merely a collection of symptoms, but a story woven through the fabric of lives. It tells a tale of inequality, discrimination, and a lack of access to quality mental health care.

In Black women, the symptoms of MDD often paint a more acute and sorrowful picture. The typical symptoms, such as persistent sadness, loss of interest in once-loved activities, and changes in appetite and sleep patterns, merge with an often-heightened sense of worthlessness and hopelessness.[8] These emotional caverns are deeper, wider, and more difficult to traverse.

Why this increased prevalence? Why these more profound manifestations? The answer is neither simple nor singular, but a mosaic crafted from various elements.

First, through the historical lens, the legacy of slavery, segregation, and discrimination has left scars that continue to ache. The collective memory of

---

7   Yucel, Aylin, Swarnava Sanyal, Ekere James Essien, Osaro Mgbere, Rajender R. Aparasu, Vinod S. Bhatara, Joy Alonzo et al., 2019. "Racial/ethnic Differences In Treatment Quality Among Youth With Primary Care Provider-initiated Versus Mental Health Specialist-initiated Care For Major Depressive Disorders," *Child and Adolescent Mental Health* (25), 1:28–35. doi.org/10.1111/camh.12359.

8   Beauboeuf-Lafontant, Tamara, 2007. "You Have To Show Strength," *Gender & Society* (21), 1:28–51. doi.org/10.1177/0891243206294108.

pain and subjugation forms the background against which individual suffering plays out. The echoes of a wounded past reverberate in the psyche, creating an environment ripe for the growth of MDD.

Generational trauma and racism, these ancient and insidious foes, have cast a somber pall on the hearts and minds of Black women. Together, they weave a tale of sorrow, where echoes of the past resonate in the present, shaping the very fabric of the soul. Their influence on the increased incidence of major depressive disorder (MDD) in Black women is profound, complex, and deserving of thoughtful exploration.

In the depths of generational trauma lies the history of a people. Slavery, discrimination, violence—these are not merely chapters in a history book, but wounds carried in the very DNA, passed down from generation to generation. It is a pain not easily forgotten, an ache that continues to reverberate, altering perceptions, attitudes, and emotional well-being.

This trauma molds the mind into a fortress, with thick walls built to protect while simultaneously imprisoning. Inside these walls, despair festers, nurturing the seeds of MDD. These emotional scars shape the way Black women perceive the world and themselves, leading to a sense of hopelessness and worthlessness that finds its manifestation in depression.

Racism—the relentless and pervasive storm—adds to this melancholy narrative. It is the cold wind that chills the soul and the rain that seeps into the bones. In the daily lives of Black women, racism is often an uninvited companion, shaping experiences, limiting opportunities, and draining the spirit.

The subtle and overt expressions of racism, whether in the workplace, healthcare system, or social interactions, pile up like stones, heavy and unyielding. These stones press on the heart and soul, creating an environment where MDD can flourish. It is a garden where the thorns of prejudice and discrimination overshadow the flowers of happiness and self-worth as they struggle to bloom.

Racism is not just an external force; it permeates the psyche, altering self-perception and self-worth. It's a distorted mirror reflecting a world that often devalues and diminishes the identity and experiences of Black women. This altered reflection can lead to a profound sense of isolation and despair, feeding the vicious cycle of MDD.

Moreover, the mental health of Black women has been profoundly affected by various unfair laws and practices that have emerged and persisted throughout history. These discriminatory policies have not only limited opportunities and access to vital resources, but have also created chronic stressors that can lead to mental health conditions like anxiety, depression, and major depressive disorder (MDD).

One of the primary causes of fatigue, particularly in recent years, has been the high incidence of housing discrimination. This often manifests in a practice known as redlining, where banks and insurance companies refuse or limit loans, mortgages, and insurance within specific geographic areas that predominantly affect Black communities. As a result, many Black women have been forced to live in underfunded and neglected neighborhoods, impacting their mental well-being through increased stress, reduced access to healthcare, and diminished educational opportunities. Unfair rental practices also lead to discrimination in housing rentals and have limited Black women's ability to move into safer and more prosperous neighborhoods, reinforcing cycles of poverty and contributing to feelings of hopelessness and depression.

An additional burden presents itself for Black women in the form of employment discrimination. They have historically been paid less than their white counterparts for the same work. In the United States, Black women typically earned only a fraction of what white men earned for similar work. According to data from the US Census Bureau and other sources, Black women, on average, earned approximately sixty-one to sixty-three cents for every dollar earned by white, non-Hispanic men. This gap seems even larger when you consider the earnings of white women. While they earn more than Black women, they face their own wage gap relative to white men.

Several factors contribute to this wage gap, including occupational segregation (being concentrated in lower-paying jobs), differences in educational attainment, and direct discrimination in hiring, promotions, and pay. The gap is often even wider for older Black women and those in higher-paying occupations and industries.[9]

The wage gap's persistence reflects broader systemic inequalities, and has tangible impacts on the economic security and overall well-being of Black women and their families. These financial disparities can also contribute to stress and other mental health issues, further highlighting the need for comprehensive efforts to understand and address the underlying causes of the wage gap. This wage disparity not only affects economic stability, but also creates feelings of injustice, chronic stress, and anxiety. For those who need additional resources and support due to these disparities, the results can be even more bleak. Some policies have made it harder for Black women to access public assistance.[10] This creates barriers to essential resources like food, housing, and healthcare. Such limitations also contribute to chronic stress and anxiety, amplifying mental health challenges.

9   "Equal Pay Day: March 14, 2023." 2023. US Census Bureau. www.census.gov/newsroom/stories/equal-pay-day.html.

10   Michener, Jamila and Margaret Brower, 2020. "What's Policy Got To Do With It? Race, Gender & Economic Inequality In the United States," *Daedalus* (149), 1:100–118. doi.org/10.1162/daed_a_01776.

For Black women who do ascend onto the leadership track in corporate America, there is also a "glass ceiling." And more recently, studies show they are also encountering a "glass cliff." The term describes the barriers Black women and other people of color face to advancing in the workplace. Research shows that women and people of color are more likely to be appointed to poorly performing companies than white males.[11] Limitations on promotions and career advancement contribute to feelings of frustration and worthlessness, which may lead to MDD.

In addition, Black women often experience disparities in healthcare access and treatment. Implicit biases within the healthcare system can lead to misdiagnosis, undertreatment, or a lack of access to mental health services, further exacerbating mental health conditions. Black women in the United States also suffer disproportionately from maternal mortality. According to the Centers for Disease Control (CDC), Black women are three times more likely to die from a pregnancy-related cause than white women. Multiple factors contribute to these disparities, such as variation in quality healthcare, underlying chronic conditions, structural racism, and racial prejudice.[12] The fear, grief, and stress associated with this can have long-lasting mental health impacts.

For Black women who grew up in predominantly Black neighborhoods, predominantly Black schools often receive fewer resources. Lack of access to quality education not only limits economic opportunities, but also contributes to feelings of marginalization and hopelessness, potentially leading to mental health issues. Predominantly Black neighborhoods are also statistically more likely to be heavily policed, which leads to a higher

11 Ellis, Terry. 2022. " 'Very rarely is it as good as it seems': Black women in leadership are finding themselves on the 'glass cliff.' " CNN. www.cnn.com/2022/12/17/us/black-women-glass-cliff-reaj/index.html.

12 "Working Together to Reduce Black Maternal Mortality | Health Equity Features." 2023. CDC. www.cdc.gov/healthequity/features/maternal-mortality/index.html.

likelihood of Black people being stopped, arrested, convicted, and sentenced, and of receiving longer sentences than their white counterparts.[13] The disproportionate arrest and incarceration of Black individuals affects Black women both directly and indirectly. Those who are incarcerated face trauma and mental health challenges, while those with incarcerated family members experience stress, financial hardship, and emotional strain.

It might appear that the solution to many of these challenges is for Black women to become more civically involved by voting. However, according to the League of Women Voters, Black women have played pivotal roles in voter mobilization and voter turnout for years. More than two-thirds of Black women turned out to vote in the 2020 presidential election—the third highest rate of any race or gender group.[14] In addition, laws that disproportionately affect Black communities' ability to vote[15] can lead to feelings of disenfranchisement and powerlessness, contributing to broader feelings of marginalization and despair. Studies show that a higher rate of felony voter disenfranchisement in the Black community is also likely to have consequences for population health and overall health equity.[16]

The cumulative effect of these unfair laws and practices is a complex web of disadvantage, discrimination, and despair. They create an environment where mental health issues can flourish and access to help is limited or nonexistent. By recognizing and addressing these systemic barriers, society

13 Goff, Phillip Atiba, Matthew O. Jackson, Brooke A. L. Di Leone, Carmen M. Culotta, and Natalie Ann DiTomasso, 2014. "The Essence Of Innocence: Consequences Of Dehumanizing Black Children." Journal of Personality and Social Psychology (106), 4:526–545. doi.org/10.1037/a0035663.

14 "The power of us: Black women deciding elections." 2022. League of Women Voters. www.lwv.org/newsroom/news-clips/power-us-black-women-deciding-elections.

15 Tensley, Brandon. 2021. "Black voting rights and voter suppression: A timeline." CNN. www.cnn.com/interactive/2021/05/politics/black-voting-rights-suppression-timeline/.

16 Homan, Patricia and Tyson H. Brown, 2022. "Sick and Tired Of Being Excluded: Structural Racism In Disenfranchisement As A Threat To Population Health Equity," Health Affairs (41), 2:219–227. doi.org/10.1377/hlthaff.2021.01414.

can create a pathway toward mental wellness, social justice, and equality for Black women. And for Black women, part of the individual path to healing should involve acknowledgment of how much these laws affect them in the society they navigate. The resulting impact on the mental health and emotional well-being of Black women should not be understated.

The dance between generational trauma and racism is a complex and sorrowful waltz. Together, they craft an environment rife with stressors that is uniquely positioned to foster MDD. They entwine, one feeding the other, in a symbiotic relationship that fuels depression. Yet, understanding this relationship and recognizing the profound ways in which generational trauma and racism impact the mental health of Black women is the first step toward healing. It's the dawning light that can pierce the shadow in a search for understanding for Black women to heal themselves.

This understanding calls for empathy, compassion, and action. It calls for a mental health care system that acknowledges these unique challenges and provides culturally sensitive treatment. It calls for societal change where the roots of racism are confronted and the echoes of generational trauma are met with empathy and support. It also calls for Black women to empower themselves with more knowledge of the benefits of mental health treatment in conjunction with ancestral and communal methods for self-care.

Next is the societal stage. Systemic racism and inequality continue to impact the lives of Black women, molding their daily existence into a crucible of stress and adversity. Unequal access to healthcare, education, and economic opportunities feeds the roots of depression. Societal judgment, often misunderstood or dismissed, builds walls around the soul, leaving many Black women isolated in their struggle.

Furthermore, the intersectionality of gender and race compounds these challenges. Black women bear the dual burden of racism and sexism, an intersection where oppression multiplies. Their identities as women have an impact on their experiences, in addition to the color of their skin. The societal expectations and roles assigned to them often lead to a complex array of emotional challenges, giving MDD fertile ground to take root.

Kimberlé Crenshaw, a scholar and civil rights advocate, introduced the term "intersectionality" in the late 1980s. Her groundbreaking concept has illuminated our understanding of identity, discrimination, and social dynamics, particularly in the lives of Black women. Through the lens of intersectionality, we gain an in-depth view of how various aspects of identity interconnect and compound, shaping daily experiences and mental well-being.

Crenshaw's definition of intersectionality recognizes that individuals don't exist within a single categorization but rather at the nexus of various social identities, such as race, gender, class, and sexuality.[17] It is the intersection of these factors that creates a unique and complex web of experiences. These intersections don't simply add to one another, but often multiply, creating amplified, multifaceted forms of discrimination.

Intersectionality, a concept as complex and multi-layered as the human experience it seeks to define, emerges as a critical framework to understand the unique struggles of Black women, particularly in relation to major depressive disorder (MDD). It's a prism through which the overlapping identities—race, gender, and class—refract, creating a spectrum of experiences that transcends the sum of its parts. Within this kaleidoscopic perspective, the intricate relationship between intersectionality and MDD in Black women unfolds like an intricate puzzle, riddled with challenges, yet filled with insight.

---

17   Nash, Jennifer C., *Black Feminism Reimagined: After Intersectionality*, New York, USA: Duke University Press, 2019. https://doi.org/10.1515/9781478002253.

Black women stand at the crossroads of identities, where the paths of race and gender converge. These are not mere lines on a chart, but dynamic forces that shape lives, mold perceptions, and exert pressure. They form a complex intersection where experiences are amplified and vulnerabilities are heightened.

At this intersection, the weight of racism and sexism does not merely add up; it multiplies. The burden becomes more than the sum of its parts, an intensified experience that affects both the internal psyche and the external world. This amplification creates fertile ground for MDD, a place where despair finds its voice and hope often struggles to be heard.

Race and gender, in the context of Black women, do not exist in isolation but are entangled with the strings of socioeconomic status, education, and access to healthcare. These intersections create a maze where navigating the path to well-being becomes increasingly complex. The interplay of numerous inequalities frequently hides the very tools necessary to combat MDD—access to mental health care, socioeconomic stability, and social support—within this maze.

Consider the workplace, where the double bind of racism and sexism can lead to a perpetual battle, a relentless struggle to prove one's worth. The daily microaggressions, the silent judgments, the glass ceilings—they converge into a storm, a tempest that wears down the spirit, eroding self-esteem and nourishing the roots of depression.

In the realm of healthcare, intersectionality plays out in a similarly complex dance. The challenge is not merely accessing care, but finding care that understands and recognizes the unique experiences of Black women. Culturally insensitive healthcare can turn the path to healing into a path of further alienation, pushing MDD into the shadows, where it grows unseen but deeply felt.

Within the familial sphere, Black women often play a pivotal role as the core of family and community. The pressure to be strong and to shoulder the burdens of others can become a crushing weight. The very strength that is celebrated becomes a double-edged sword, leading to an internalization of pain and a reluctance to seek help. These feelings are also often heightened by embracing or at least identifying with societal, gender, and race-based schema that dictate actions. One of the most harmful is that of the "Strong Black Woman," which is so much a part of US culture that it is seldom realized how great a toll it has taken on the emotional well-being of the African American woman. As much as it may give her the illusion of control, it keeps her from identifying what she needs and reaching out for help.[18]

Issues related to African American women's intersecting race-gender identities affect their stress experience, coping responses, and mental health.[19] The Strong Black Woman (SBW) is a race-gender schema that prescribes culturally specific feminine expectations for African American women, including unyielding strength, the assumption of multiple roles, and caring for others.[20] Media, parents, and communities socialize African American women to internalize and accept the SBW schema.[21] Among African American women, the notion of "strength" is a central theme in their identities.[22] Although the SBW schema is rooted in African American

18 Romero, R. E. (2000). The icon of the strong Black woman: The paradox of strength. In L. C. Jackson & B. Greene (Eds.), Psychotherapy with African American women: Innovations in psychodynamic perspective and practice (pp. 225–238). The Guilford Press.

19 Woods-Giscombé, Cheryl L. "Superwoman schema: African American women's views on stress, strength, and health." Qualitative health research 20, no. 5 (2010): 668–683.

20 Settles, Isis H., Jennifer S. Pratt-Hyatt, and NiCole T. Buchanan. "Through the lens of race: Black and White women's perceptions of womanhood." Psychology of Women Quarterly 32, no. 4 (2008): 454–468.

21 Stanton, Alexis G., Morgan C. Jerald, L. Monique Ward, and Lanice R. Avery. "Social media contributions to strong Black woman ideal endorsement and Black women's mental health." Psychology of Women Quarterly 41, no. 4 (2017): 465–478.

22 Abrams, Jasmine A., Morgan Maxwell, Michell Pope, and Faye Z. Belgrave. "Carrying the world with the grace of a lady and the grit of a warrior: Deepening our understanding of the 'Strong Black Woman' schema." Psychology of Women Quarterly 38, no. 4 (2014): 503–518.

women's strength and resilience, it is linked to adverse mental and physical health outcomes such as cardiovascular disease.[23]

The emergence of the SBW schema can be attributed to several factors. The origins of the SBW schema date back to slavery.[24] The portrayal of African American women as physically and psychologically stronger than European American women, and equal to African American men, enabled European Americans to justify their enslavement and inhuman treatment.[25] Enslaved African women, in turn, socialized African American girls to be strong to prepare them for the often brutal and violent life on the plantations.[26] Post-enslavement, the systemic oppressions against African American women and their families limited their access to resources[27] and contributed to the need for these women to be strong.[28]

Over the last decade, with a large percentage of African American households headed by a single mother[29] and African American men being incarcerated at a high rate,[30] many African American women have been forced to assume the roles of financial provider, caregiver, and community agent.[31]

23 Harrington, Ellen F., Janis H. Crowther, and Jillian C. Shipherd. "Trauma, binge eating, and the 'strong Black woman.' " Journal of consulting and clinical psychology 78, no. 4 (2010): 469.

24 Abrams, et al., , "Carrying the world with the grace of a lady and the grit of a warrior: Deepening our understanding of the "Strong Black Woman" schema."

25 Harrington, et al., "Trauma, binge eating, and the "strong Black woman."

26 West, Lindsey M., Roxanne A. Donovan, and Amanda R. Daniel. "The price of strength: Black college women's perspectives on the strong Black woman stereotype." Women & Therapy 39, no. 3–4 (2016): 390–412.

27 Collins, Patricia Hill. Black sexual politics: African Americans, gender, and the new racism. Routledge, 2004.

28 Woods-Giscombé CL. Superwoman schema: African American women's views on stress, strength, and health. Qual Health Res. 2010 May;20(5):668-83. doi: 10.1177/1049732310361892. Epub 2010 Feb 12. PMID: 20154298; PMCID: PMC3072704.

29 Collins, Patricia Hill. Black feminist thought: Knowledge, consciousness, and the politics of empowerment. Routledge, 2009.

30 "Trends in US corrections." Fact Sheet, The Sentencing Project. Washington, DC (2020).

31 Romero, 2000.

Moreover, it has been theorized that the SBW schema was initially developed within the Black community and churches as an alternative to the negative stereotypes of African American women in the United States culture,[32] which included the domineering Sapphire, the hypersexual Jezebel, the nurturing, asexual Mammy for European American families, and the dependent Welfare Queen.[33]

The SBW schema consists of emotional regulation, caretaking of African American families, and being economically independent, traits that may counteract the negative stereotypical images of African American women.[34] Lastly, lessons from foremothers, personal histories of disappointment (e.g., being let down by family members or friends) or abuse, and spiritual values (e.g., faith gave them the strength to overcome challenges without other's help) also contributed to the emergence of the SBW schema.

In qualitative interviews, some African American women perceived the SBW schema as empowering.[35] However, Black feminist scholars have theorized that the schema is actually a controlling image that justifies these women's lived experience and limits their ability to cultivate a healthy sense of self-acceptance and a positive sense of self.[36] Other theorists also suggest that this role is simply another stereotype that places responsibility on African

---

32   Beauboeuf-Lafontant, Tamara. "Keeping up appearances, getting fed up: The embodiment of strength among African American women." *Meridians: feminism, race, transnationalism* 5, no. 2 (2005): 104–123.

33   Collins, 2009.

34   Nelson, Tamara, Esteban V. Cardemil, and Camille T. Adeoye. "Rethinking strength: Black women's perceptions of the "Strong Black Woman" role." *Psychology of women quarterly* 40, no. 4 (2016): 551–563.

35   Woods-Giscombé, 2010.

36   Speight, Suzette L., Denise A. Isom, and Anita Jones Thomas, ' From Hottentot to Superwoman: Issues of Identity and Mental Health for African American Women', in Elizabeth Nutt Williams, and Carolyn Zerbe Enns (eds), *The Oxford Handbook of Feminist Multicultural Counseling Psychology, Oxford Library of Psychology* (2012; online edn, Oxford Academic, 21 Nov. 2012), https://doi.org/10.1093/oxfordhb/9780199744220.013.0006.

American women while concealing structural institutions that maintain racial inequality.[37] African American women frequently deem the SBW schema ideal in spite of these criticisms.[38]

According to the SBW framework, there are benefits as well as drawbacks associated with this schema. Perceived benefits include cultivating a positive self-image, a sense of self-efficacy, and a commitment to caring for families. The schema is also perceived to help with the survival of the self (e.g., survive in society in spite of oppressions and perceived inadequacy of resources) and the African American family and community. Despite these benefits, the SBW facade may mask African American women's internal struggles[39] such as hopelessness and depression.[40] The SBW schema is associated with strain in interpersonal relationships (e.g., their self-reliance may make others feel unneeded) and stress-related health behaviors such as emotional eating and smoking. Many African American women eventually realize that the costs of the SBW schema outweigh its benefits.[41] Indeed, recent literature has highlighted the association between the SBW schema and negative mental health.[42]

In a recent study, researchers examined the relationship between the "Strong Black Woman" (SBW) schema and psychological outcomes such as depression, anxiety, and loneliness among African American women. African American women were more likely to report depression symptoms than

---

37 Collins, 2009.

38 Dow, Dawn Marie. "Negotiating 'the welfare queen' and 'the strong Black woman' African American middle-class mothers' work and family perspectives." Sociological Perspectives 58, no. 1 (2015): 36–55.

39 Collins, 2000.

40 Blackwell, Debra L., Jacqueline W. Lucas, and Tainya C. Clarke. "Summary health statistics for US adults: national health interview survey, 2012." Vital and health statistics. Series 10, Data from the National Health Survey 260 (2014): 1–161.

41 Woods-Giscombé, 2010.

42 Donovan, Roxanne A., and Lindsey M. West. "Stress and mental health: Moderating role of the strong Black woman stereotype." Journal of Black Psychology 41, no. 4 (2015): 384–396.

European American women. African Americans and Caribbean Black women also often experience anxiety disorders and symptoms. Loneliness was positively associated with depressive and anxious symptoms among African American women, and the SBW schema was found to predict depressive symptoms and was associated with anxiety symptoms.

Coping responses and self-compassion were examined as potential mediators between the SBW schema and psychological health. However, coping responses were found to be mediators rather than moderators in the relationship between perceived racism and health outcomes.[43] Self-compassion, which involves viewing oneself with kindness and non-judgment, was negatively associated with depression and loneliness.[44] The study hypothesized that self-compassion may mediate the link between the SBW schema and psychological health.

Overall, the study highlights the impact of the SBW schema on the mental health of African American women. The findings suggest that the SBW schema may contribute to feelings of depression, anxiety, and loneliness. Maladaptive perfectionism, consisting of unrealistically high expectations and overly critical self-evaluations,[45] coping responses, and self-compassion, were identified as potential mechanisms through which the SBW schema influences psychological health outcomes. Further research is needed to

43 Clark, Rodney, Norman H. Anderson, Vernessa R. Clark, and David R. Williams, 1999. "Racism As a Stressor For African Americans: A Biopsychosocial Model." American Psychologist (54), 10:805–816. doi.org/10.1037/0003-066x.54.10.805.

44 Chau, Anson C.M., Suzanne Ho-wai So, Xiaoqi Sun, Chen Zhu, Chui-De Chiu, Raymond C.K. Chan, and Patrick S.C. Leung, 2022. "The Co-occurrence Of Multidimensional Loneliness With Depression, Social Anxiety and Paranoia In Non-clinical Young Adults: A Latent Profile Analysis," Frontiers in Psychiatry (13). doi.org/10.3389/fpsyt.2022.931558.

45 Woodfin, Vivian, Per-Einar Binder, and Helge Molde, 2020. "The Psychometric Properties Of the Frost Multidimensional Perfectionism Scale—Brief," Frontiers in Psychology (11). doi.org/10.3389/fpsyg.2020.01860.

better understand these relationships and develop interventions to support the mental well-being of African American women.[46]

The path to healing, likewise, is obscured by obstacles. Stigmatization around mental health within the community, coupled with a lack of culturally sensitive healthcare, often turns the road to recovery into a labyrinth. For Black women, the paths to depression are many and winding, filled with the sharp stones of systemic racism and the mire of cultural stigmatization. It's a journey undertaken with burdens that are uniquely and disproportionately heavy, laden with the pressures of supporting family and community and navigating a world that often appears oblivious to their pain.

In the arena of PTSD, the narrative shifts to one of survival, resilience, and unspoken trauma. The trauma that stems from violence, both witnessed and experienced, can leave indelible scars that stretch across time. PTSD, with its intrusive memories and shattered sense of security, manifests as a cruel reminder of a past that refuses to remain buried. It is a ghost that haunts; a wound that refuses to heal.

Like shadows lengthening at dusk, post-traumatic stress disorder (PTSD) casts a long and darkening pall over the lives it touches. Among Black women, its prevalence and effects are pronounced and profound, sculpted by the unique intersectionality of their lived experiences.

PTSD is a silent specter, often dwelling unseen within the minds of its bearers, born of trauma and brought to life by the brain's struggle to navigate distress. It manifests in myriad ways, creating a mosaic of symptoms as varied as the individuals it affects. Black women wrestling with PTSD may find themselves caught in the tightening coils of recurring memories, nightmares, and flashbacks. They might navigate the quicksand of sleep disturbances, concentration issues, and an avoidance

---

46 Liao, Kelly Yu-Hsin, Meifen Wei, and Mengxi Yin, 2019. "The Misunderstood Schema Of the Strong Black Woman: Exploring Its Mental Health Consequences And Coping Responses Among African American Women," *Psychology of Women Quarterly* (44), 1:84–104. doi. org/10.1177/0361684319883198.

of reminders of the traumatic events during their waking hours, as well as intense emotional distress, fear, and hypervigilance.

Yet, the tale of PTSD in Black women is not merely a clinical list of symptoms. It is a narrative woven with threads of systemic racism, sexism, and the emotional inheritance of generational trauma. They stand at the intersection of multiple forms of discrimination, and it is in this confluence that the risk of PTSD burgeons.

The pernicious tendrils of systemic racism and sexism entwine in the lives of Black women, predisposing them to higher levels of trauma. Exposure to violence, discrimination, and poverty heightens the risk of PTSD, and the unique position of Black women at the crossroads of these societal stressors illuminates their increased susceptibility.

Take, for example, the racial profiling and police violence disproportionately experienced by Black individuals and communities. These create not only immediate trauma, but also an ongoing fear for personal and familial safety. This chronic dread can foster a state of hypervigilance, a cornerstone of PTSD.

Black women stand at the poignant intersection of race and gender, bearing the weight of both their Blackness and womanhood in a world that often seems intent on diminishing both. When violence, racial profiling, and police brutality erupt in their communities, these eruptions don't simply dissipate; they reverberate, leaving aftershocks of anxiety and post-traumatic stress disorder (PTSD) that echo throughout their lives.

Like silent ripples disturbing a tranquil pond, violence and racial profiling disturb the mental peace of Black women, gradually cultivating the harsh seeds of anxiety. The unpredictable nature of these societal issues adds to the stress and fear of the next incident, creating an insidious, chronic worry. This persistent state of heightened alertness and worry is the crux of anxiety disorder.

Moreover, violence and police brutality specifically act as traumatic stressors. They are unexpected, violent disruptions that shatter the illusion of safety. For Black women who directly experience, witness, or even hear about such incidents, these experiences can be deeply distressing and traumatic, leading to the onset of PTSD.

PTSD, in this context, is a beast with many heads. It lurks in the form of nightmares, flashbacks, and intrusive thoughts about the violent incident. It skulks in day-to-day life, creating avoidance behavior where the sufferer may go to great lengths to evade reminders of the trauma. It is a constant, unwelcome companion, causing the sufferer to startle easily, have sleep disturbances, and experience angry outbursts.

Additionally, police brutality and violence against Black individuals heighten the sense of racial identity among Black women and the constant threat it seems to be under. This "racial trauma" or "race-based traumatic stress injury" can be a powerful contributor to the development of anxiety and PTSD, a reality etched in the psyche of those constantly living under its shadow.

Even indirect exposure to violence and police brutality, such as through media reports, can lead to vicarious trauma, and it too can sow the seeds of anxiety and PTSD. This exposure amplifies the narrative that Black lives are under constant threat, thereby increasing vigilance, distress, and fear.

The mental health of Black women is significantly affected by the phenomenon of Linked Fate. Linked Fate refers to the recognition that individual life chances are interconnected and influenced by systemic racism and discrimination. This concept plays a crucial role in shaping the experiences and mental well-being of Black women due to the intersectionality of their identities.

Black women face the compounded effects of racism and sexism, which contribute to their unique challenges and experiences of violence and discrimination. The experience of discrimination has been linked to negative mental health outcomes, including increased levels of stress, anxiety, depression, and psychological distress.

The persistent racial disparities in health, with Black individuals experiencing higher mortality rates than their white counterparts, further highlight the detrimental impact of racism on mental health.

The concept of Linked Fate fosters a collective consciousness among Black individuals, leading to a strong sense of racial and gender identification. This collective consciousness can provide a sense of community and support, but it can also contribute to increased stress and pressure. Black women may feel a responsibility to advocate for the well-being of their community, which can lead to emotional exhaustion and burnout.

The experience of Linked Fate can also result in a heightened awareness of racial discrimination and injustice, leading to increased vigilance and hypervigilance in navigating daily life. Black women may constantly be on guard, anticipating and preparing for potential encounters with racism and discrimination. This state of hypervigilance can be mentally and emotionally draining, contributing to chronic stress and anxiety.

Furthermore, the persistence of racial disparities and the added burden of racism contribute to the mental health challenges faced by Black women.[47] The cumulative effects of experiencing discrimination and witnessing racial injustices can lead to a sense of hopelessness, anger, and frustration. These emotions can further exacerbate mental health issues and contribute to feelings of powerlessness and despair.

It is important to note that the mental health experiences of Black women are not uniform, as individuals within this group have diverse backgrounds and experiences.[48] Intersectionality recognizes the complexity of identities

---

47 Williams, David R. and Selina A. Mohammed, 2008. "Discrimination and Racial Disparities In Health: Evidence And Needed Research," *Journal of Behavioral Medicine* (32), 1:20–47. doi. org/10.1007/s10865-008-9185-0.

48 Williams and Mohammed, 2008.

and experiences within the Black community, highlighting the need for an individualized and nuanced approach to mental health support.

So, the mental health of Black women is significantly affected by the phenomenon of Linked Fate. The intersectionality of their identities, compounded by their experiences of racism and sexism, contributes to unique challenges and mental health disparities. In addition to fostering a sense of community, Linked Fate can also increase stress and pressure. The heightened awareness of racial discrimination and the persistence of racial disparities further impact mental well-being. Recognizing the diverse experiences within the Black community and adopting an intersectional approach to mental health support is crucial to addressing the mental health needs of Black women.

Similarly, Black women often bear the burden of stereotypes and prejudices that originate from the intersection of their racial and gender identities. The resulting discrimination and microaggressions are traumatic stressors that can ignite the fuse of PTSD, leaving its sufferers to grapple with the repercussions.

Furthermore, the generational trauma carried by Black women—the echo of centuries of slavery, segregation, and systemic racism—reverberates through their mental health. This enduring trauma, passed down like a haunting refrain, has the potential to prime the psyche for PTSD, adding another layer to its complex etiology.

Access to mental health care, an essential instrument for healing, is unfortunately not on a level playing field. Structural barriers, stigma, and a lack of culturally sensitive care often impede Black women's path to treatment, allowing PTSD to dig its roots deeper.

The journey of PTSD among Black women is a poignant tale of resilience in the face of systemic adversity. It is the story of battling unseen demons while navigating the tangible challenges of societal discrimination. As we seek to understand this narrative, we must endeavor to address the underlying societal inequities and offer culturally informed, empathetic care. In this effort lies the hope for healing, empowerment, and a future where Black women are not disproportionately burdened by the weight of PTSD.

Black women, warriors in a battle that is often unseen, face PTSD's relentless grip with a courage that is both admirable and heartbreaking. Their resilience, however, does not diminish the need for intervention. Society must play its part in assuaging this malady, for ignoring it is akin to denying the validity of their struggle.

The mental health of Black women and their ability to seek care for mental illnesses like MDD and PTSD are significantly impacted by structural barriers that contribute to a lack of mental health support and resources in the Black community. These barriers arise from systemic racism, socioeconomic disparities, and cultural factors that intersect to create unique challenges for Black women's mental well-being.

Structural barriers, such as limited access to affordable and culturally competent mental health services, contribute to disparities in mental health outcomes for Black women. The scarcity of mental health providers who understand the specific experiences and needs of Black women can result in misdiagnosis, inadequate treatment, and a lack of culturally appropriate interventions.[49] This lack of representation and understanding can lead to feelings of alienation and mistrust, further deterring Black women from seeking help.

---

49 Hammond, Wizdom Powell, 2012. "Taking It Like a Man: Masculine Role Norms As Moderators Of The Racial Discrimination–depressive Symptoms Association Among African American Men," *American Journal of Public Health* (102), S2:S232-S241. doi.org/10.2105/ajph.2011.300485.

Socioeconomic disparities also play a significant role in limiting mental health support for Black women. Economic inequality and limited resources can restrict access to quality healthcare, including mental health services.[50] The financial burden of seeking treatment, coupled with the lack of insurance coverage, can create barriers to accessing necessary care. Additionally, the intersectionality of race and gender can compound these challenges, as Black women often face employment discrimination and wage disparities, further limiting their ability to afford mental health services.

Cultural factors within the Black community can also contribute to the lack of mental health support. Stigma surrounding mental health issues persists, leading to a reluctance to seek help due to fears of judgment and social repercussions.[51] The strong emphasis on strength and resilience within the Black community can discourage individuals, particularly Black women, from acknowledging and addressing their mental health needs. The pressure to conform to societal expectations of strength and self-reliance can prevent Black women from seeking support and expressing vulnerability.

Furthermore, the historical and ongoing experiences of racism and discrimination contribute to the mental health challenges faced by Black women. Racial trauma, microaggressions, and systemic racism can lead to chronic stress, anxiety, and depression.[52] The cumulative effects of these experiences can result in a range of mental health issues, including post-traumatic stress disorder (PTSD) and racial battle fatigue. The lack of mental health support exacerbates the impact of these experiences, leaving Black women without the necessary resources to heal and recover.

50   Hammond, 2012.

51   Chatters, Linda M., Robert W. Taylor, Amanda Toler Woodward, and Emily J. Nicklett, 2015. "Social Support From Church and Family Members And Depressive Symptoms Among Older African Americans," *The American Journal of Geriatric Psychiatry* (23), 6:559–567. doi. org/10.1016/j.jagp.2014.04.008.

52   Hammond, 2012.

Addressing the structural barriers to mental health support for Black women requires a multifaceted approach. It involves increasing access to affordable and culturally competent mental health services, improving the representation of Black mental health professionals, and destigmatizing mental health within the Black community.[53] Community-based initiatives, such as support groups and outreach programs, can provide safe spaces for Black women to seek support and share their experiences. Additionally, addressing the socioeconomic disparities that limit access to mental health care is crucial, including advocating for policies that promote equitable healthcare and economic opportunities for Black women.

Addressing these barriers requires a comprehensive approach that includes increasing access to culturally competent care, destigmatizing mental health, and addressing the socioeconomic disparities that limit access to mental health services. By dismantling these barriers, we can create a more inclusive and supportive environment for the mental well-being of Black women.

One therapist who is working to create these types of environments is Ashley McGirt, MSW, LCSW, a racial trauma therapist and founder of WA/CA Therapy Fund Foundation. She explains[54] how racial trauma compounds the challenges of seeking mental health therapy for Black people, especially due to the dearth of Black mental health providers:

> Well, your story is my story. It is the story of so many other Black women, so many other Black people who look like us and are presented with these challenges. When I was young, my grandmother passed away, and I experienced grief that turned into major depression. I ended up seeing a counselor who was a white woman, and she did not understand the role of grandmother[s] in Black families. She didn't understand anything about

53 Hammond, 2012.

54 McGirt, Ashley. "Black Mental Health Matters." Interview by Elizabeth Leiba. Black Power Moves, EBONY Covering Black America Podcast Network, January 18, 2022. open.spotify.com/episode/6ZMCKxycFzqslscOWPsaTI?si=w3x5RvrUTNigMtgDO5TT1A.

Black culture. Here I was, educating this white woman on Black life; on the intricacies of race, relationships, at nine years old.

I actually wanted to be a lawyer. I was really obsessed with the law, and I just knew that was the path that I wanted to take. But through the experience of losing my grandmother and having these sessions with this white woman who didn't understand me, I told my mom what was going on. She searched and searched and tried to find a Black therapist for me, and she didn't.

[...] I experienced a huge bout of depression. I'm like, "There's got to be other Black children, other Black people, who are experiencing these things. And we should not have to spend our therapy session educating the counselor on what life is like for Black people in America." So, I did a whole three-sixty.

I still love the law. I still do a lot of work...[related to] criminal justice [and] ending mass incarceration, but ultimately, I wanted to understand depression, suicidal ideation. My research is on African American suicide because I suffered from those things. I didn't want to live when my grandmother passed away. I didn't understand death. [...] I do a lot of work around death and dying. I also ended up being a hospice therapist, and the majority of my Black hospital patients were extremely young, like my grandmother, who died at sixty-two years old. My grandmother passed [away] from a stroke. The leading cause of stroke is stress. What is it about the Black community that we are so stressed? Well, racism, systemic oppression, all these different things, and I'm a social justice advocate at my core.

Dr. Jessica Elizabeth Isom, MD, is a full-time psychiatrist, clinical instructor at Yale University, and attending psychiatrist at Boston Medical Center. She advocates[55]

55   Isom, Jessica. "Breaking the Rules of Engagement on Racetalk." Interview by Elizabeth Leiba. Black Power Moves, EBONY Covering Black America Podcast Network, June 18, 2022. open.spotify. com/episode/1YD0e9JS8EzInKJwqImsh6?si=5B74gpicRhuqlxM3924yhQ.

for the importance of culturally competent mental health services and treatment that extend beyond simply pathologizing the mental illness of Black patients:

...throughout my professional journey, it's been a very interesting experience, to say the least, of Blackness mostly being pathologized in ways that I couldn't put language to until I went to public health school, and that's where I learned that the reason why Blackness is listed as a risk factor, for example, all these different organ systems, and like medical issues, the reason why is because of racial racism, not necessarily because of race, so [it] kind of added a larger context, like a bigger lens through which to view medicine. And the more I zoomed out and added in that context, the more I realized that there needed to be a focus that wasn't focused around these people. There's something going on with them. There's something wrong with them, and we need to help them. And more so, "Oh, these people are not being served in a number of different ways and we need to improve the services that we offer."

So now I was very much focused on, "Okay. How do I take my education and my training and all the value in that and then kind of weed out the stuff that's not useful?" And then I have to fill it in with something else, because if I see a healthcare professional, I want to have a different experience. I want my mom to, etc., etc. So I realized that there's not a lot of people in this specific area focusing in this space. And now it's 1 or 2 percent of psychiatrists who are Black. You know, [if] we're not going to do it, who else will? So in that 2 percent, most of us are thinking about and focused on, how do we serve our own communities? [...] We've experienced our training and we see how there's shortcomings in how, as a collective, psychiatrists and other mental health professionals practice. So it's kind of impossible not to focus our attention on our own community. For all of those reasons, there's just a lot of work to do.

In short, the descriptive landscape of mental health among Black women is a poignant blend of resilience and despair. It is a painting filled with shadows and light, where the hues of suffering and strength mingle. The complexity of this landscape is not a mere academic pursuit, but a call to action. We must turn our eyes toward solutions, toward a world where mental health is not an isolated island but an integrated part of well-being. We must cultivate understanding, empathy, and compassion for ourselves. Our communities must forge pathways that lead not only to treatment but also to prevention, to a future where mental health is not a privilege but a right. In the dance between pain and healing, between darkness and light, lies a path to a better future. For Black women and for our community as a whole, we must have the courage to walk this path together. Only then will the echoes of despair transform into a symphony of hope.

journaling questions

1. How do you perceive the impact of generational trauma on your mental health and emotional well-being? How have you addressed or started to heal this form of trauma in your life?

2. In what ways do you feel racism has impacted your psyche and mental health? How do you work toward acknowledging and addressing these impacts?

3. How do you understand the intersection of race and mental health disorders like major depressive disorder (MDD) and post-traumatic stress disorder (PTSD)? How has this understanding shaped your approach to mental health care?

4. How has the "Strong Black Woman" schema affected your perception of your mental health needs? What steps can you take to dismantle this harmful narrative?

5. How does the concept of "Linked Fate" impact your mental health, particularly in terms of hypervigilance and fear? How can you address these impacts in a healing and nurturing way?

6. What structural barriers have you faced in seeking mental health support? How have these barriers influenced your journey toward emotional well-being?

7. How has your experience been in finding representative, culturally sensitive mental health care? How important is this aspect of care to you, and why?

8. Have you encountered stigma or negative judgments associated with seeking mental health care? How do you navigate or challenge these stigmas?

9. How have socioeconomic factors impacted your access to mental health care? How do you navigate these challenges?

10. How can community support and self-advocacy play a role in overcoming structural barriers and stigma related to mental health care? How can you encourage these supportive systems in your own life and within your community?

affirmations

1. I acknowledge the generational trauma in my lineage, and I am committed to healing and breaking the cycle for myself and future generations.

2. I recognize the deep-seated effects of racism on my psyche, and I am actively working toward healing these wounds.

3. I acknowledge the racial components in mental health disorders, and I am actively seeking understanding and healing in a way that respects my unique experiences as a Black woman.

4. I release the burden of the "Strong Black Woman" schema, acknowledging my right to vulnerability, support, and care.

5. I am aware of the impact of Linked Fate on my mental well-being. I am cultivating resilience, safety, and peace in the face of this collective experience.

6. Despite the structural barriers I face, I am determined to seek and obtain the mental health support I deserve.

7. I deserve mental health care that is culturally sensitive and representative. I will strive to find it and advocate for it.

8. I stand against the stigma of seeking mental health care. My journey to healing is valid and necessary.

9. Despite socioeconomic challenges, I am resourceful and determined to seek access to the mental health care I need.

10. I am worthy of healing, care, and peace. I will advocate for myself and my mental health needs, knowing that I am deserving of wellness and joy.

systemic and multifaceted mental health issues in the Black community

"I think it's really important to take the stigma away from mental health... My brain and my heart are really important to me. I don't know why I wouldn't seek help to have those things be as healthy as my teeth."

—Kerry Washington

In the tapestry of our shared human experience, the subject of mental health is a thread that weaves its way through every fold. The psychological well-being of a community bears immeasurable significance in defining its essence, vitality, and future. Like an orchestra in a harmonious symphony, a community thrives when every participant can play their part in health and happiness. However, the Black community's access to adequate mental health resources has historically been and remains a discordant note in this rousing symphony.

Historically, mental health care in the United States has been markedly deficient for people of color, particularly the Black community. Through the bleak corridors of time, stigma, underfunding, and the disturbing disruption of systemic racism have deterred access to mental health resources. While overall public acceptance of mental health care has surged forward, the proportion of accessible resources for the Black community lags stubbornly behind.

Consider the sparse representation of Black mental health practitioners. According to recent data collected by the American Psychological Association, a mere 4 percent of psychologists in the US are Black.[56] It's like expecting a single candle to illuminate an entire city at night; the enormity of the task renders the limited resource almost futile. This lack of representation not only presents a logistical problem, it also hinders the essential ingredient of understanding—the cultural sensitivity required to provide effective mental health care.

For the Black community, particularly Black women, the intersections of race, gender, and mental health create a unique conundrum. Black women juggle societal expectations, cultural norms, and systemic oppression. The result is a potent cocktail of stressors that amplifies their need for culturally sensitive mental health care. To borrow a phrase from the Harlem Renaissance

---

56 "How diverse is the psychology workforce?" n.d. American Psychological Association. Accessed August 6, 2023. www.apa.org/monitor/2018/02/datapoint.

poet Langston Hughes, these stressors are the "dream deferred," the burden that "sags like a heavy load." Yet, the existing system often fails to meet their unique needs.

The daunting task of rectifying this inequity demands our immediate and deliberate attention. Affordable, culturally sensitive, and accessible mental health care must take precedence on our collective agenda. Strategies should include increasing federal funding for mental health resources in predominantly Black communities and incentivizing the training of more Black mental health practitioners.

Now, more than ever, the world is in a state of flux and tension. In the face of a global pandemic and surging social upheaval, mental health issues have found fertile ground to flourish. The pressures exerted upon the Black community have only been magnified in these extraordinary times, amplifying the importance of this mission. Like a clarion call in the midst of a storm, the need for significant change rings out.

To undertake this task is to walk the path toward healing, not just present-day, but also historical wounds. It is to acknowledge the tales of hardship etched into the spirit of the Black community, and to make a conscious choice to foster and nurture resilience instead of perpetuating suffering. This is more than an aspiration—it is an imperative. We are, after all, in pursuit of the promise of health and happiness for all. As the poet Maya Angelou once wrote, "Out of the huts of history's shame, I rise." Now is the time to ensure that the Black community, too, can rise.

Dr. Wizdom Powell, PhD, Chief Social Impact and Diversity Officer at Headspace and clinical psychologist, agrees that there is a pressing need to empower the Black community to create, receive, and embrace pathways for mental healthcare with accessible skills, strategies, and tools to navigate the trauma we experience daily.

I think that we have not really honored the tried-and-true traditions of becoming well in Black communities. We have been healing radically for four hundred plus years since 1619, and the fact that we are still here and not just here, like just existing, means that we're thriving in some ways, even with all of the onslaught of racialized violence and degradation, we are still moving and shaking, and contributing to a world. Imagine a world without us in it. Like, I can't.

We are doing so much daily to heal, grow, and thrive, and I think the first thing we have to do is honor those traditions, air them out, share those with the world, because people don't get, how is it that they're still here and still active and engaged and smiling at each other. How are we doing that? There's wisdom that we need to share with the world.

The first narrative change—this idea that Black folk don't want to get well, or that we don't want to pay attention to our mental and emotional wellness, doesn't really square up with all of the healing work we've been doing over time.

Secondly, we have to start having different conversations in our community about what constitutes strength. This idea that we're supposed to leap over structural disadvantage, racialized violence, [and] systematic oppression in a single bound. It's mythic, like superheroes are. We need to really start telling ourselves the truth about who we are and what we are here to do, [which] is to experience a range of emotions from anger to sadness to shame [to] disappointment. All of those are valid, and we have to honor that and hold space for those emotional experiences.

Third, we need to be helping each other find the pathways to those supports earlier on, so I'm really, really passionate about youth mental health, because if we don't fight for them, then our children, their children's children, and their children will have to do the work that we avoided.

Times have changed. But we have to still honor those traditions, and more importantly, we have to make it okay for us to have those issues. Stop telling people that they should push through adversity. Or when someone asks you, "How are you doing, Queen?" and you go, "Well, you know how I'm doing. I'm making it." Tell the truth and shame the devil! Tell folks how you're really doing, so folks can show up for you in the ways that we should show up for one another.[57]

Unseen, unheard, and often veiled in a shroud of silence and misunderstanding, mental health has long been a subject relegated to the margins in many communities. Yet none so deeply as in the Black community, where the stigma adheres with adhesive tenacity, insidiously shaping perceptions and barring access to critical resources. Within this intricate tapestry, Black women find themselves at a potent intersection, bearing the weight of this stigma while navigating the unique challenges posed by systemic racism and sexism.

The stigma surrounding mental health in the Black community is as multifaceted as it is deep-rooted. Historic misuse and mistrust of the healthcare system, cultural norms that prize stoicism and resilience, and a society that often overlooks the mental health needs of Black women all contribute to the stigmatization. This makes it harder for Black women to seek help, perpetuating a cycle where silence feeds stigma and stigma feeds silence.

Yet, within the silence, there are whispers of change. As we peel back the layers of mental health stigma, the path toward holistic healing and wellness comes into focus. A holistic approach embraces not only the mind, but also the body and spirit. It is not a mere absence of mental illness; it is a continuous practice of nurturing one's complete well-being. This concept is far from alien

57 Powell, Wizdom, 2022. "Healing Trauma to Improve Emotional Wellbeing in Black Communities." Interview by Elizabeth Leiba. EBONY Covering Black America Podcast Network. open.spotify.com/episode/2qEOeysSzZm9de7t5SU8sA?si=1ef9cfac33ab47d0.

to the Black community, resonating with the ancestral wisdom that speaks to interconnectedness and community healing.

Framing mental health within this holistic paradigm taps into the roots of ancestral strength and resilience that have guided Black communities through centuries of adversity. It promotes the understanding that mental health is not a standalone entity, but an essential facet of overall health and well-being. It underscores the recognition that mental health is not a personal failing, but a collective responsibility affected by societal structures and systemic forces.

This paradigm shift allows us to highlight how structural racism not only impacts socioeconomic conditions but also seeps into the psychological well-being of Black women, engendering stress, anxiety, depression, and PTSD. It raises the imperative need to dismantle these harmful structures to pave the way for true mental wellness.

This reframing of mental health creates a safe space for dialogue where experiences can be shared and understood without judgment. It validates seeking support as a testament to strength rather than a sign of weakness. It encourages healing practices that include traditional therapy, community support, self-care, and other therapeutic techniques that align with the cultural values and realities of Black women.

More importantly, destigmatizing mental health care in the Black community illuminates a pathway to healing that honors ancestral wisdom while addressing contemporary struggles. It elevates the narrative that mental health care is not merely an act of crisis management but a radical act of self-preservation, resistance, and affirmation of life.

To liberate mental health from the confines of stigma is to empower Black women to take ownership of their healing journey, to allow them to bear witness to their struggles, but also to their individual and collective power. It is an ongoing act of resistance against systemic forces that neglect their mental health. And in doing so, we weave a narrative of strength, resilience, and healing that is deserving of Black women and their mental wellness.

In the process of empowering ourselves to take control of the narrative and practices around our own mental health and well-being, it is important to understand the historical context. Taking care of our spirits, nurturing our sense of self, and leaning on the power of the collective have always been integral parts of our wellness practice as Black women, since antiquity.

One way to further these discussions and understandings is to explore alternative treatment methods rooted in ancestral traditions from across the African diaspora. A rich tapestry of holistic practices dating back thousands of years offers an array of strategies, from herbal remedies and spiritual rituals to communal therapies and physical exercises. These practices have provided holistic approaches to mental health care and are relevant to the modern Black woman in her search for more comprehensive and culturally sensitive methods of healing.

For instance, the practice of Ubuntu, originating from Southern Africa, is a philosophy that promotes the belief in a universal bond of sharing that connects all humanity. Ubuntu can be understood as the belief in the interconnectedness and interdependence of all individuals within a community. It emphasizes the idea that one's humanity is defined through their relationships with others. The term "Ubuntu" is derived from the Zulu and Xhosa languages, and can be translated as "I am because we are" or "humanity toward others." It encompasses values such as compassion, empathy, respect, and communalism.

The principles of Ubuntu can encourage open dialogue and community support as essential components for maintaining mental health. In African societies, mental health is often viewed holistically, encompassing not only the individual but also their relationships and community. Ubuntu promotes a sense of belonging and social connectedness, which are crucial for mental well-being.

By embracing Ubuntu, individuals are encouraged to engage in open dialogue and communication, fostering a supportive environment where they can express their thoughts, emotions, and challenges without fear of judgment or stigma. This open dialogue allows for the sharing of experiences, the validation of emotions, and the development of coping strategies. Ubuntu also emphasizes the importance of community support, where individuals come together to provide assistance, guidance, and encouragement to those in need.[58]

Furthermore, Ubuntu promotes a sense of collective responsibility for the well-being of others. This communal approach to mental health encourages individuals to actively support and care for one another, reducing feelings of isolation and promoting a sense of belonging. Ubuntu recognizes that mental health is not solely an individual concern, but a collective responsibility.

This collective ethos encourages open dialogue and community support as essential components for maintaining mental health. The principles of Ubuntu could be integrated into mental health practices by fostering supportive networks for Black women, spaces where they can express their struggles and find mutual understanding and healing.

Similarly, African tradition recognizes the healing power of storytelling, an ancient practice where life experiences are shared and wisdom is passed down through generations. Storytelling serves as a tool for providing instruction, building community, nurturing the spirit, and sustaining a unique culture. Likewise, African American storytelling serves a higher purpose than conveying information or responding to a question. Storytelling develops connections

58   Mthombeni, Zama Mabel, 2022. "Xenophobia In South Africa," *The Thinker* (93), 4:63–73. doi. org/10.36615/the_thinker.v93i4.2207.

between people and ideas, serving as one of the most important traditions within both African and African American cultures. It connects African Americans through their shared culture, history, and ideals. By sharing stories of mental health discovery and practice in person, online, and in community spaces, the process of destigmatizing help-seeking can flourish.

Particularly since the COVID-19 pandemic, there has been an increase in online spaces dedicated to Black women sharing their stories of healing and taking care of their mental health. There are organizations that have made it much easier for Black women to get connected. For example, "Therapy for Black Girls," founded by Joy Harden Bradford, PhD, compiles a useful directory of therapists, produces a podcast, publishes a weekly newsletter, and hosts a free weekly support group.

"Inclusive Therapists" provides therapists with racial trauma training to ensure health care providers look at mental health holistically. The organization has a directory of professionals, and many of them offer reduced-price virtual sessions. In addition, online support groups like Sista Afya's free virtual conversations make sharing experiences easier and more accessible. Their group sessions focus on how to reclaim your time, create boundaries, and prioritize rest in a world that praises accomplishments.

Ethel's Club, a Brooklyn-based wellness group, centers people of color and hosts virtual group healing and grieving sessions twice a month. And if you're interested in using tarot and astrology in your mental health journey, "Dive in Well" has a variety of programs in addition to donation-based therapy classes and wellness-focused workshops. Finally, for an LGBTQ+ therapist of color, "LGBTQ Psychotherapists of Color" has a directory that also serves as a vital resource for the community.[59] By integrating these practices of sharing communal space and storytelling into

59   Barbour, Shannon. 2020. "Accessible Mental Health Resources for Black Women." *Cosmopolitan.* www.cosmopolitan.com/health-fitness/a32731463/mental-health-resources-for-black-women/.

modern therapy, Black women can find healing in familiar experiences and lessons of their ancestors.

Another example of a beneficial traditional strategy is the use of indigenous healing practices. Indigenous healing systems rooted in African cultural traditions have been shown to be relevant to mental health in the African diaspora. These healing practices, which include rituals, ceremonies, and the use of herbal remedies, contribute to emotional well-being and healing.[60] Indigenous healing systems are deeply connected to the cultural and social contexts of indigenous peoples, and they offer unique perspectives on resilience and mental health.

Resilience, as understood in indigenous perspectives, goes beyond individual traits and includes relational, ecocentric, and cosmocentric concepts of self and personhood. These concepts emphasize the interconnectedness of individuals with their communities and the natural world, highlighting the importance of social support and a sense of belonging for emotional well-being and healing. Indigenous healing practices also involve revisiting collective history to valorize collective identity, revitalizing language and culture as resources for narrative self-fashioning and healing, and renewing individual and collective agency through political activism and empowerment.[61]

Indigenous healing systems provide additional resources for coping with emotional distress and can be integrated into mental health care.[62] These systems offer holistic approaches that address the physical, mental, and spiritual

60 Whaley, Arthur L., 2020. "Associations Between Seeking Help From Indigenous Healers and Symptoms Of Depression Versus Psychosis In The African Diaspora Of The United States," *Counselling and Psychotherapy Research* (21), 1:179–187. doi.org/10.1002/capr.12313.

61 Kirmayer, Laurence J., Stéphane Dandeneau, Elizabeth P. Marshall, Morgan W. Phillips, and Karla Jessen Williamson, 2011. "Rethinking Resilience From Indigenous Perspectives," *The Canadian Journal of Psychiatry* (56), 2:84–91. doi.org/10.1177/070674371105600203.

62 Lee, Boon-Ooi, 2023. "Journeying Through Different Mythic Worlds," *International Perspectives in Psychology* (12), 2:96–111. doi.org/10.1027/2157-3891/a000072.

dimensions of health. For example, in Ghana, indigenous healing focuses on the "whom" instead of the "what" way of healing, considering factors such as angry ancestors, evil spirits, or bewitchment as potential causes of illness. Indigenous healing practices also involve detailed history taking, physical examination, and divination to make diagnoses.[63]

The relevance of indigenous healing systems to mental health in the African diaspora has been supported by research. Studies have shown that seeking help from indigenous healers can have a positive role in the mental health functioning of individuals with less severe mental health problems. Indigenous healing practices may be protective against certain mental health problems, and their effects may depend on the severity of psychopathology for which help is sought. Openness to discussing indigenous healing practices in the context of Western counseling and psychotherapy facilitates cultural competence and can contribute to mental health promotion and policy.

However, it is important to note that the impact of indigenous healing practices on mental health outcomes should be examined further through treatment outcome studies. Comparative research would provide more definitive evidence of the role of indigenous healing practices in addressing mental health disparities.[64] Collaboration between indigenous healing systems and Western biomedical health systems can be strengthened through accurate understandings of the different stakeholders involved.[65]

Additionally, ancestral healing practices like dance and drum therapies, common in many African societies, have been found to have therapeutic effects, facilitating

63   Nare, Neo and David D. Mphuthi, 2018. "Conceptualisation Of African Primal Health Care Within Mental Health Care," *Curationis* (41), 1. doi.org/10.4102/curationis.v41i1.1753.

64   Whaley, 2020.

65   Kpobi, Lily and Leslie Swartz, 2019. "Indigenous and Faith Healing In Ghana: A Brief Examination Of The Formalising Process And Collaborative Efforts With The Biomedical Health System," *African Journal of Primary Health Care & Family Medicine* (11), 1. doi.org/10.4102/phcfm.v11i1.2035.

emotional release and promoting well-being. The transmission of knowledge in South African traditional healing practices identifies drumming and dancing as one of the six disciplines of traditional healing, along with divination, herbs, control of ancestral spirits, the cult of foreign *ndzawe* spirits, and the training of new sangomas, who are traditional healers in South Africa.[66] The sangomas' healing rituals are considered incomplete without the use of drumming and dancing. These rituals involve the calling up of ancestral spirits through dance, music, and drumming, suggesting that these practices have a therapeutic role in traditional healing. Incorporating such ancestral practices into modern mental health care provides an integrative approach that not only treats the symptoms but also addresses the whole person—mind, body, and spirit.

Another supplement to traditional mental healthcare is the incorporation of self-recovery practices. Black women have historically engaged in self-recovery movements, recognizing the need to heal themselves from the effects of institutionalized racism, sexism, and capitalist oppression.[67] These movements emphasize the importance of self-care, self-reflection, and self-empowerment as essential components of emotional well-being. By politicizing the self-recovery movement, Black women have reclaimed their agency and actively worked toward their own healing.[68]

Tricia Hersey founded the Nap Ministry in 2016, which is another well-known contemporary online community that reflects this movement. Her organization offers virtual or Atlanta-based guided sessions of "rest coaching" and "spiritual direction."[69] She urges followers to devote the time they might otherwise use for extra work to sleeping instead—the stretches they'd spend staring at a screen to

66 Thornton, Robert, 2009. "The Transmission Of Knowledge In South African Traditional Healing," *Africa* (79), 1:17–34. doi.org/10.3366/e0001972008000582.

67 hooks, bell and Bell Hooks, 1995. "Sisters Of the Yam: Black Women And Self-recovery." *African American Review* (29), 3:529. doi.org/10.2307/3042416.

68 hooks and Hooks, 1995.

69 Barbour, 2020.

staring into space. Tense moments given over to worrying about disappointing others would be better spent reflecting on their own needs and comforts.[70]

Additionally, the concept of racism-related stress and its impact on well-being is relevant to understanding the mental health experiences of Black women. Racism-related stress refers to the stressors and challenges that individuals of color face due to systemic racism and discrimination. This conceptualization takes into account the larger social and historical context and recognizes the mediating role of culture-based variables in the relationship between racism and well-being.[71] Understanding and addressing racism-related stress is crucial for promoting the mental health and emotional well-being of Black women.

Incorporating these ancestral methods of mental health care is essential for the modern Black woman in her pursuit of holistic well-being. By embracing indigenous healing practices, engaging in self-recovery movements, and addressing racism-related stress, Black women can reclaim their cultural heritage, strengthen their resilience, and promote their emotional well-being. These practices provide a comprehensive and culturally sensitive approach to mental health care that acknowledges the unique experiences and needs of Black women.

In her quest for holistic mental health practices, the Black woman of today can find solace and strength in the wisdom of her ancestors and practices unique to the experience of Black women in America. By understanding the prevalence of mental health illness, recognizing the cultural uniqueness of her struggles, and drawing upon the wealth of ancestral knowledge and practices, she equips herself to walk a path toward healing. After all, in the words of Maya Angelou,

70   McAfee, Melonyce. 2022. "The Nap Bishop Is Spreading the Good Word: Rest." *The New York Times.* www.nytimes.com/2022/10/13/well/live/nap-ministry-bishop-tricia-hersey.html.

71   Harrell, Shelly P., 2000. "A Multidimensional Conceptualization Of Racism-related Stress: Implications For the Well-being Of People Of Color." *American Journal of Orthopsychiatry* (70), 1:42–57. doi.org/10.1037/h0087722.

protecting my peace

"The ache for home lives in all of us. The safe place where we can go as we are and not be questioned."[72]

And with the words of the ancestor, we also have an obligation to pay that forward by encouraging the next generation to understand the importance of nurturing their mental health. The road to acceptance and understanding is a winding one, also connected to generational trauma and adopted norms to counter the cruel reality of racism in society.

For centuries, the experience of the African American community has been steeped in a potent brew of resilience, survival, and faith. Historical injustices, societal pressures, and cultural norms have shaped the complex relationship with mental health at the center of this story. The deep-rooted tendrils of Christianity frequently conceal an underlying mistrust toward mental health treatment as a result of this dynamic interaction.[73]

In the African American community, historical events have left indelible marks on the collective psyche. The repercussions of slavery, segregation, and systemic racism echo in the halls of memory, breathing life into narratives of mistrust and suspicion. Mental health institutions, once tools for oppression and misdiagnosis, have become symbolic edifices of fear and misunderstanding. As James Baldwin wrote, "People are trapped in history, and history is trapped in them." This history has cast long, oppressive shadows on the mental health landscape, engendering an atmosphere of mistrust.

Historical experiences of racism and discrimination have contributed to a deep-rooted mistrust among marginalized communities, including Black Americans, toward the healthcare system. This mistrust is often based on a history of

72   Angelou, Maya. "All God's Children Need Traveling Shoes." New York: Random House, 1986.

73   Hankerson, Sidney H. and Myrna M. Weissman, 2012. "Church-based Health Programs For Mental Disorders Among African Americans: a Review," *Psychiatric Services* (63), 3:243–249. doi. org/10.1176/appi.ps.201100216.

medical exploitation, unethical research practices, and unequal treatment.[74] Regarding the concept of cultural mistrust among African Americans and its impact on mental health service utilization, Whaley argues that cultural mistrust, rooted in historical experiences of racism and discrimination, can contribute to the underutilization of mental health services by African Americans. This suggests that historical factors, such as systemic racism, can shape individuals' attitudes and behaviors toward healthcare.[75]

Overlaying this mistrust is the tapestry of Christianity, an enduring force in the African American community. Amidst the trials and tribulations, it has been a beacon of hope and a haven of solace. From the sorrowful plantation songs to the powerful sermons of Black churches, faith has carried African Americans through the raging tempests of injustice.

Yet, within this framework, the conventional understanding of mental health has been traditionally viewed through the prism of spirituality. Mental health issues, rather than being recognized as medical conditions, have often been relegated to the realms of spiritual warfare, tests of faith, or the consequences of moral failing. This perspective can unintentionally perpetuate the stigma associated with mental illness and discourage the pursuit of professional mental health care.

Given the centrality of the church in African American communities, it's not uncommon to find those grappling with mental health issues seeking solace within the hallowed halls of faith before turning to mental health practitioners. To paraphrase W. E. B. Du Bois, the church in the African American community is not just an ecclesiastical institution but a social one as well, offering solace for the spirit and the mind.

---

74 Bogart, Laura M., Bisola O. Ojikutu, Keshav Tyagi, David C. Klein, Matt G. Mutchler, Lu Dong, Sean Jamar Lawrence et al., 2021. "Covid-19 Related Medical Mistrust, Health Impacts, and Potential Vaccine Hesitancy Among Black Americans Living With HIV," *JAIDS Journal of Acquired Immune Deficiency Syndromes* (86), 2:200–207. doi.org/10.1097/qai.0000000000002570.

75 Whaley, Arthur L., 2001. "Cultural Mistrust and Mental Health Services For African Americans," *The Counseling Psychologist* (29), 4:513–531. doi.org/10.1177/0011000001294003.

This reality does not discredit the therapeutic value of faith-based support. However, it emphasizes the need to foster dialogue, weave mental health literacy into the communal narrative, and bridge the gap between faith and mental health care. Engaging church leaders in mental health advocacy, for instance, could help transform the church into a conduit for promoting mental health resources.

In addition to bridging the gap between the church and mental health literacy, there is also an urgent need to bridge the gap between our youth and mental health awareness. In the regal theater of life, youth is the first act of promise and potential. For Black youth, however, their debut to the world can become a haunting performance under the weight of systemic racism, cultural misunderstanding, and increasing mental health concerns. As the number of young lives interrupted by the tragic specter of suicide grows, addressing the mental health of Black youth ascends the staircase of urgency.

Young people constantly encounter reminders that they will experience discrimination based on the color of their skin at school, on social media, and in society at large. For Black youths, this burden is not just detrimental to their mental health—it is potentially deadly.

Black children (under thirteen) are almost twice as likely to die by suicide as their white peers, according to the US Surgeon General's Advisory on Protecting Youth Mental Health in 2021.[76] The Centers for Disease Control and Prevention (CDC) confirmed that suicide rates for Black youths (ages ten to twenty-four) rose significantly from 2018 to 2021.[77] Compounding the issue, Black Americans face barriers to care that make it harder to seek help, and the stigma of discussing mental health challenges adds an additional hurdle.

76   "The US Surgeon General's Advisory." 2021. HHS.gov. www.hhs.gov/sites/default/files/surgeon-general-youth-mental-health-advisory.pdf.

77   Stone, Deborah.M, Karin A Mack, and Judith Qualters, 2023. "Notes From the Field: Recent Changes In Suicide Rates, By Race And Ethnicity And Age Group—United States, 2021," MMWR. Morbidity and Mortality Weekly Report (72), 6:160–162. doi.org/10.15585/mmwr.mm7206a4m https://www.cdc.gov/mmwr/volumes/72/wr/mm7206a4.htm.

What can be done to halt and begin to reverse the harm that is being done? There is no simple, one-size-fits-all solution. A broad, coordinated approach is necessary. Practical strategies might include culturally sensitive mental health education in schools, bolstering the representation of Black mental health practitioners, and implementing mentorship programs. These strategies could serve as protective layers, softening the blow of life's harsh realities and empowering Black youth to face their struggles with resilience and hope.

But in order to get started, it's essential to understand the issues at play and our options for resolving them.

Black youths are at a higher risk for depression, anxiety, and other mental health struggles than their non-Black peers. The CDC reported that suicide is increasing at a faster rate for Black youths than it is for any other racial or ethnic group (36.6 percent from 2018 to 2021).[78] High-profile suicides in the Black community this past year have drawn further attention to the issue.

These issues cannot be traced back to one specific source; racial discrimination, financial and institutional barriers to care, and police killings of Black Americans are just some of the many contributing factors.

Similarly, there is not one specific solution. Getting mental health care may seem like a good place to start, but Black youth are likely to encounter systemic barriers. Cost is often a prohibitive factor. Unfortunately, even those who can handle the cost may not have access. The United States is struggling with a shortage of therapists. And then it comes down to the quality of care provided: Most clinicians are white, which means that it is difficult for Black Americans to find culturally competent care. Speaking with a culturally sensitive therapist is often key when youth are healing from racial trauma.

~~~~~~~~

78   Stone et al., 2023.

But Black youths may never be encouraged to seek help in the first place; caregivers and educators often fail to recognize their struggles due to a lack of understanding of how mental health issues present in teens and young adults of different races, ethnicities, and backgrounds. Black youths may demonstrate warning signs in different ways than other young people—ways that are often interpreted as behavioral problems rather than trauma, anxiety, or depression. As a result, a punitive approach is taken: Black youths exhibiting symptoms of mental health challenges are more likely to be suspended from school, expelled, or sent into the juvenile justice system.

Intersectionality—a lens that helps us understand the way multiple forms of inequality intersect and compound—also plays a role in mental health because our other identities may change how we experience the world. For example, Black youth who are also transgender or nonbinary face a higher risk of suicide than those with only one marginalized identity. This illustrates how the intersection of various identities presents new challenges for many youths, challenges that need to be considered when supporting large-scale reform.

Many of the hurdles outlined above can only be removed through large-scale structural reform. However robust, this work must also drill down to address the unique lived experiences and perspectives of Black youths; evidence-based solutions must include a racially heterogeneous lens as comprehensive as they themselves are. And it must be acknowledged that the responsibility should not, and does not, rest solely on parents and caretakers, much less young people themselves.

Therefore, we must turn to community-based solutions that reach individuals where they are and when they need them most. With so many systemic issues at play, only a robust and collective effort can make a difference.

First, the role of mental health practitioners is akin to that of the lighthouse keeper, guiding distressed vessels through tumultuous waters. An increase in

Black mental health practitioners can foster trust by providing culturally attuned care that understands the unique struggles Black youth face. An important first step is improving access to mental health care, particularly culturally competent care. This is easier said than done, especially given the therapist shortage, but it can be facilitated through a number of avenues. Schools, for one, must become safe havens for students, with suicide intervention programs and strong support systems for Black students. Schools are one of the most effective environments for early intervention because that is where young people spend the majority of their time. They can play a pivotal role by becoming epicenters of mental health literacy.

Incorporating age-appropriate and culturally responsive mental health education into the curriculum could demystify mental health and challenge stigma. To borrow a phrase from poet Audre Lorde, "For the master's tools will never dismantle the master's house." New tools—empathy, knowledge, resilience—need to be fostered to dismantle the house of stigma and misunderstanding. Of course, for this to work, the education system must also address its history of discrimination.

More work must also be done to make higher education affordable and accessible for all. This would not only help ease the shortage of mental health care experts trained in culturally responsive care, it would also make sure Black youths have an equal opportunity to pursue their interests and passions. Advocating for scholarship programs that give Black youth the chance to study medicine, psychiatry, psychology, and social work is a step in the right direction.

The field of medicine must also evolve. Historically, most psychiatric research has been done by and for white people, leaving a profound knowledge gap that continues to endanger Black Americans. Additionally, research topics proposed by Black scientists are less likely to be funded than topics proposed by their white counterparts—a loss to the scientific community as a whole. Society must work to promote and fund research that looks at risk factors as well as protective factors, stressors, and disparities unique to Black youths in order to fully understand the obstacles they face and how to address them.

Finally, funding social programs and resources that uplift the Black community will foster a sense of belonging and support. Programs that reach all young people, especially those that address economic inequality, can help establish protective factors for Black youth. Community building is a strong, well-established method for suicide prevention and improving youth mental health.[79]

All these steps are necessary if we are going to help the many youth of color who feel their lives are not worth living. Yet the significance of mental health is more than a tapestry of statistics. It is the unseen music, the unheard rhythm, that orchestrates their lives and affects their worldviews, dreams, and potential. The contemporary era, the age of social media, compounds the complexity of the issue. On the one hand, social media is the digital agora, the communal hearth where young minds gather, sharing dreams and shaping identities. On the other hand, it can be a double-edged sword, exposing Black youth to cyberbullying, racism, and unrealistic societal standards. This digital paradox breeds anxiety, depression, and feelings of isolation, compounding existing mental health concerns.

In light of these challenges, addressing the mental health of Black youth is like nurturing a precious sapling in the face of a storm. The tree must be cared for, protected, and reinforced to withstand the tempest. It necessitates the creation of safe spaces where young minds can unravel their worries and share their experiences without fear of judgment or misunderstanding.

In the dawn of a new era, prioritizing the mental health of Black youth is not just a moral imperative; it is an investment in a future of promise and potential.

~~~~~~~~~

79 "To Support Black Youth Mental Health, We Must Look to Community-Based Solutions." 2023. The Jed Foundation. jedfoundation.org/to-support-black-youth-mental-health-we-must-look-to-community-based-solutions/.

It involves making mental health a community-wide conversation, a dialogue that transcends the boundaries of fear and stigma. As we navigate these troubled waters, let us remember that in our hands lies the power to transform these challenges into stepping stones toward a more empathetic, understanding, and resilient society. As Langston Hughes wrote, "Hold fast to dreams, for if dreams die, life is a broken-winged bird that cannot fly." Let us endeavor to keep the dreams of our Black youth alive.

In the final analysis, understanding the mental health perceptions within the African American community necessitates navigation through the intricate maze of historical scars, cultural norms, and the faith tapestry. It requires an unwavering commitment to address the mistrust, a reevaluation of the traditional narratives, and a delicate balancing of faith and medicine. As with the delicate artistry of quilt-making, each square of knowledge, understanding, and advocacy we add brings us closer to a more holistic, compassionate mental health paradigm for the African American community. In this tapestry, the past, present, and future intertwine, each thread a silent vow of healing and growth.

For Black women, the goal must also include a journey of self-care, self-compassion, and self-love. In the exquisite tapestry of life, Black women have long been the unspoken heroines, the invisible seamstresses weaving together the fabric of communities and families. Often, they bear the dual burdens of societal expectations and systemic injustices, weathering the storm with grace and resilience. However, in this formidable dance, the drumbeat of responsibility frequently drowns out the rhythm of self-care.

Black women, I implore you to honor the sacred space within, to dance to the melody of self-care, and to permit yourselves the grace of rest. The African proverb says, "You cannot pour from an empty cup." Indeed, self-care is not an act of indulgence but an essential lifeline, a replenishing spring that fortifies you against life's adversities.

Imagine self-care as a lush garden within you. To flourish, this garden requires tending, watering, and ample sunlight. Prioritizing your emotional well-being is akin to the careful nurturing of this garden, allowing your inner flora to bloom with vibrancy and strength.

Speak to yourself with the gentle caress of a love song. Your internal dialogue shapes your reality. In the reflection of self-love, every obstacle is surmountable, and every challenge is a stepping stone. Even when the world roars with criticism, let your inner voice whisper words of encouragement and validation, and affirmation. Remember, you are a symphony of strength, a sonnet of resilience, and a poem of perseverance.

Be kind to yourself. Amid the turbulence of life, this act of kindness serves as your anchor. Like the ebbs and flows of the ocean tide, allow yourself the room to make mistakes, to retreat, to regroup, and to surge forward again. In this dance, there is no misstep, only the rhythm of learning and growth.

In the pursuit of self-care, rest is your faithful companion. It's the restorative pause in the melody of the beautiful, yet sometimes overwhelming, symphony of life. To rest is not to concede defeat but to honor your humanity, recharge your energy, and revive your spirit. As the brilliant Maya Angelou wrote, "Every person needs to take one day away." So, permit yourself a day, an hour, or a moment to simply be, to breathe, and to exist.

Black women, in you lies a wellspring of power and resilience. Yet even the mightiest river requires a source, a space of tranquility, and replenishment. Prioritize self-care, honor your emotional well-being, and take solace in the sweet embrace of rest. Each step you take toward nurturing yourself is a step toward a future filled with vitality and fulfillment.

In this journey, let the words of Toni Morrison echo in your hearts: "You are your best thing." Indeed, you are. Cherish yourselves, nurture your spirits, and let the glow of self-love illuminate your path. As you journey onward, may your steps be light, your spirit strong, and your heart filled with the timeless melody of self-care.

In the intricate musical masterpiece of life, it's essential to acknowledge that the harmonious expression of self-care has often been silenced for Black women, drowned out by the booming percussion of societal expectations and systemic pressures. However, the gentle notes of self-care are not a luxury but a necessity, a song of survival and vitality that must find its voice within the chorus of their lived experiences.

The significance of self-care is multifaceted. Like a tranquil oasis in a desert of demands, it provides Black women with a space to replenish their energy, nurture their emotional health, and fortify their mental well-being. It's a testament to their inherent worth and a recognition of their humanity beyond societal roles. In the context of a society fraught with racial and gender-based disparities, self-care becomes an act of resistance, a reclamation of control over one's well-being.

Historically, the path to self-care for Black women has been a treacherous journey, obstructed by systemic racism, socioeconomic challenges, and cultural norms. Often bearing the mantle of the "Strong Black Woman," they navigate a myriad of stereotypes, their personal needs eclipsed by the collective demand for resilience and strength. As Zora Neale Hurston wrote, "Black women are the mules of the world." Yet even the strongest mule requires rest, nourishment, and care.

Practical strategies to prioritize self-care are like stepping stones across the river of life's demands. They provide a steady path to enhanced mental health and emotional well-being.

Foremost among these strategies is the act of setting boundaries. Asserting one's limits is an exercise in self-respect and a declaration of personal worth. It may involve saying no to excessive demands, scheduling personal time in daily routines, or establishing emotional boundaries to protect mental space. Like the roots of a mighty oak tree, these boundaries offer stability and strength amidst the storm.

Meditation and mindfulness are additional tools and potent elixirs to calm the tempestuous seas of stress and anxiety. By focusing on the present moment, Black women can anchor themselves, creating a safe harbor amidst life's turbulent waves. Even a few minutes of daily mindfulness can spark a metamorphosis from a state of constant doing to a state of serene being.

Exercise and a balanced diet, while often relegated to physical health, are vital aspects of mental health and emotional well-being. Movement releases endorphins, the body's natural mood boosters, while a nutrient-rich diet nourishes the brain, fostering mental clarity and emotional balance.

Lastly, seeking professional help when needed is an act of strength, not weakness. Therapists, particularly those trained in culturally responsive care, can provide invaluable guidance in navigating mental health challenges.

Black women, in your dance with life, the rhythm of self-care must find its place. Listen to its gentle whispers, let it inspire your movements, and let it guide your steps. Prioritizing self-care is not an act of selfishness but an affirmation of your worth, a celebration of your strength, and a testament to your resilience. Remember the words of Audre Lorde: "Caring for myself is not self-indulgence; it is self-preservation, and that is an act of political warfare." Dance on, knowing that each step toward self-care is a step toward a healthier, more fulfilled you.

journaling questions

1. How have you personally confronted and overcome the stigma surrounding mental healthcare? What advice would you offer to others facing similar stigmas?

2. How have you been able to incorporate ancestral practices into your mental health journey along with traditional treatments? What has been the impact of combining these approaches?

3. What has been your experience in seeking and finding culturally representative and sensitive therapy? How has it impacted your mental health journey?

4. How have group therapy and storytelling contributed to your healing process? How do you feel when sharing and hearing stories within a supportive community?

5. How does the principle of Ubuntu resonate with your approach to mental health? How can it guide your interactions with yourself and others?

6. How has systemic racism impacted your mental health and your ability to seek and receive quality care? What strategies have you used to navigate this?

7. Have you experienced distrust in the healthcare system? If so, how have you managed this when seeking help for mental health concerns?

8. How have your religious and spiritual beliefs influenced your approach to mental healthcare? How can they serve as a resource in your healing journey?

9. How would you convey the importance of mental health to younger generations? What messages do you believe are important to pass on?

10. How have you incorporated rest and self-care into your routine? How has it influenced your emotional well-being and your perspective on mental health?

affirmations

1. I reject the stigma associated with mental healthcare. I value my mental health and see seeking help as an act of strength and self-love.

2. I honor my roots by incorporating ancestral practices along with traditional mental healthcare. Both are valuable and contribute to my holistic healing journey.

3. I deserve therapy that is culturally sensitive and representative of my lived experience. I commit to seeking such support and advocating for its importance.

4. I acknowledge the healing power of shared experiences and storytelling. I am open to the support and community offered by group therapy.

5. I embody the principle of Ubuntu, recognizing our shared humanity. My well-being is interconnected with the well-being of others.

6. I acknowledge the impact of systemic racism on my mental health. I am resilient and will continue to strive for healing and justice.

7. I will work to build trusting relationships with healthcare providers who respect and understand my experiences. I will advocate for my needs and my care.

8. My spiritual beliefs nourish my mental well-being. I honor the role of spirituality in my journey to emotional health.

9. I will share the importance of mental health with younger generations, creating a safer and more supportive future for them.

10. I acknowledge the power of rest and self-care in supporting my emotional well-being. I will prioritize these essential aspects of my mental health journey.

the importance of protecting personal peace

"Caring for myself is not self-indulgence.
It is self-preservation, and that is an act
of political warfare."

—Audre Lorde

In the relentless ebb and flow of life, amidst the daily tides of responsibilities, systemic pressures, and societal expectations, the idea of rest, emotional well-being, and self-care often recede into the background for Black women. Yet, these seemingly quiet aspects of life bear an incredible power, a potent elixir for both body and soul, essential in the long journey toward holistic health.

Rest, in its simplest form, is a respite from labor, a pause in the ceaseless rhythm of life. Yet, for Black women, it serves as a sanctuary, a quiet act of defiance in a world that often demands their constant labor and resilience. Rest is not merely the absence of activity, but the presence of peace. It renews not just the body, but also the spirit, providing space for reflection, rejuvenation, and resilience.

Emotional well-being goes hand in hand with rest. It involves acknowledging and honoring the full spectrum of emotions, from joy and love to grief and anger. It means learning to navigate emotional waters with kindness and patience, rather than judgment. For Black women, it offers a vital space to express, process, and heal from the unique emotional stresses stemming from systemic racism and gender discrimination.

Self-care, though often seen through the narrow lens of physical health, is a multidimensional concept. For Black women, it serves as a bridge between rest, emotional well-being, and physical health. It could take the form of a nourishing meal, a calming meditation session, a moment of solitude, or even a therapeutic conversation. It is an intimate dialogue with oneself, a conscious act of caring for one's own needs in a world that often prioritizes others'.

Physical health and mental health, often viewed as separate entities, are interconnected threads in the tapestry of holistic health. Just as a tree needs both roots and leaves to thrive, so do individuals need to care for both their physical and mental health. They exist in a delicate dance of mutual influence, with physical ailments often influencing mental health, and mental distress manifesting in physical symptoms. For Black women, this interconnection is critical to acknowledge and address in order to navigate the unique health disparities they often face due to systemic factors.

Understanding and prioritizing rest, emotional well-being, self-care, and the balance of physical and mental health is not a luxury for Black women; it's a necessity. These aspects equip them to withstand, resist, and challenge the systemic pressures they face daily. They are tools of empowerment, providing strength, resilience, and clarity in the face of adversity.

It is a journey of a thousand steps, a continual practice of carving out spaces for rest, honoring emotional realities, consciously engaging in self-care, and nurturing the harmony of physical and mental health. Yet, in this journey lies the beauty and strength of Black women, the resilience embedded in their spirits, and the boundless potential that unfolds when they prioritize their holistic health and well-being.

The road to prioritizing self-care, rest, and emotional well-being is not always easy; it is often dotted with challenges, both internal and external. It requires a deliberate unlearning of societal narratives that glorify constant productivity, and a dismissal of the damaging trope of the "Strong Black Woman" that leaves little room for vulnerability or respite. It demands the courage to prioritize oneself in a world that often relegates Black women's needs to the periphery.

Yet, the seeds of change are already being sown. More and more Black women are awakening to the transformative power of self-care and rest. They are reclaiming their time, their space, and their right to emotional well-being. They are resisting societal pressures, standing tall in the face of adversity, and choosing to nurture their mental health alongside their physical health.

In this shift toward a holistic vision of health, there is also a resounding call for systemic change. The onus should not be solely on Black women to navigate health disparities or overcome the mental toll of systemic racism and sexism. Rather, it is the collective responsibility of societies, institutions, and healthcare systems to ensure equitable access to mental health resources, to challenge stigmatizing narratives, and to dismantle barriers to holistic health and well-being for Black women.

In the narrative of Black women's health, the chapters of rest, self-care, emotional well-being, and the symbiosis of physical and mental health are critical. They serve as a testament to the strength of Black women, and a call to action for a world that must do better. They remind us that the health of Black women is not a footnote, but a headline.

The essence of holistic health lies in understanding that Black women are not just surviving but thriving, not just existing but truly living. It is a celebration of Black women's resilience, a recognition of their journey, and a commitment to ensuring their well-being. It is a narrative that champions rest as resistance, emotional wellness as strength, and self-care as a revolutionary act. And within these pages, we discover the profound truth: the health and well-being of Black women are indeed worthy of prioritization, recognition, and reverence.

In the bustling arena of life, amidst the maelstrom of professional ambitions and societal expectations, the concept of self-care often takes a backseat—particularly for Black women, who often tread the high wire of striving for professional success while battling the insidious forces of systemic racism and sexism. However, there lies an underestimated power in the act of self-care, an elixir that fosters resilience, balance, and inner peace.

Professional achievements, undoubtedly, are milestones of personal growth, symbols of perseverance and hard work. But when they eclipse self-care, they risk breeding a culture of burnout, constant stress, and ultimately, the erosion of holistic health. The unforgiving treadmill of relentless ambition can lead to a disconnection from one's own needs and emotional realities, straining both mental and physical well-being.

Self-care, on the other hand, is a testament to the fundamental truth: we are human first, professionals second. It recognizes the innate need to nurture the body, mind, and spirit, to replenish the inner wellsprings of strength and vitality. For Black women, self-care takes on an even more profound significance. It becomes an act of self-preservation and resistance in a world that often undervalues their health and well-being.

The notion that professional accomplishments outweigh the necessity of self-care is a myth we need to debunk. In the captivating tapestry of life, professional accolades are but a single thread. They are important, but they do not define the entirety of one's worth or happiness. And professional accomplishments certainly do not define an identity that transcends the physical and digital environments of the workplace and ascends to a mental space that elevates the authentic self, and prioritizes care. Balancing professional endeavors with self-care is not a compromise but an investment in sustainable success and fulfillment.

Moreover, prioritizing self-care does not signify a retreat from professional aspirations but signifies a redefinition of what success truly entails. It shifts the narrative from external validation to internal peace, from relentless hustle to balanced growth, from sacrificial labor to sustainable productivity. It validates the idea that success is not solely in the destination, but also in the journey, not just in achieving, but also in thriving.

When Black women prioritize self-care, they are not just nurturing their health and well-being, they are also challenging societal narratives that equate worth with work. They are redefining success on their own terms, intertwining it with self-love, balance, and mental peace. They are setting boundaries, asserting their worth beyond their professional roles, and creating space for joy, rest, and self-discovery.

In the symphony of life, professional achievements are but one melody. Self-care, rest, emotional well-being—these are the harmonies that enrich the tune, that transform it from a simple melody to a resonating anthem. For Black women, this anthem is not just a tune; it is a battle cry, a lullaby, a hymn of resistance, resilience, and radical self-love.

In the end, the narrative we need to champion is not one of relentless striving at the expense of self-care, but one of balanced growth that honors both professional aspirations and personal well-being. It is a narrative that values the journey as much as the destination, that sees strength in rest, success in balance, and power in the radical act of self-care. Only then can we truly celebrate the resilience, strength, and profound humanity of Black women.

As the narrative unfolds, it becomes imperative to delve deeper into the nuances of self-care for Black women. In this context, self-care is not merely the popularized images of bubble baths and spa days but a broader, more intricate tapestry of practices that affirm their mental, emotional, and physical health. It encompasses everything from moments of solitude and reflection, nurturing relationships, and setting boundaries, to seeking professional help for mental health issues when required.

This recalibration of priorities, from relentless professional pursuit to conscious self-care, can indeed be a formidable task. It asks of Black women to challenge deeply ingrained societal expectations and personal beliefs. It requires a radical redefinition of what it means to be successful, resilient, and worthy. Yet, it is within this daunting journey that true transformation lies, promising not just survival, but holistic thriving.

There's an empowering ripple effect that stems from prioritizing self-care. It not only positively impacts the individual but also influences the wider community. When Black women engage in self-care, they are modeling for future generations that it is possible to pursue professional success without compromising personal well-being. They are passing down a legacy that shatters harmful stereotypes, paving the way for a world where Black women's health and well-being are valued, respected, and prioritized.

The journey to prioritizing self-care is a path that meanders through fields of self-awareness, forests of resilience, and rivers of compassion. It asks of Black women to hold space for themselves, to honor their needs, to nurture their well-being amidst the cacophony of life. In this journey, self-care becomes not just an act, but a way of life, a symphony where every note is a testament to their strength, every rhythm an echo of their resilience, and every rest, a beautiful song of self-love.

Moreover, it is crucial to note that the responsibility for fostering this culture of self-care extends beyond Black women themselves. Institutions, workplaces, and societal structures must also play a significant role in facilitating an environment that not only allows but actively encourages self-care. They should strive to dismantle systemic barriers, provide resources, and create policies that acknowledge the unique struggles Black women face and support their well-being.

The call to prioritize self-care over relentless professional pursuit is more than a plea; it is a rallying cry for systemic change, a song of defiance against oppressive structures, and a celebration of Black women's resilience and strength. It champions a world where Black women's success is measured not only by their professional achievements, but also by their holistic well-being.

In prioritizing self-care, Black women chart a course that honors both their professional aspirations and their human needs, a journey that equally values their ambition and their peace. It is a journey of balance, resilience, and defiance, an ode to their strength, a testament to their courage, and a profound act of radical self-love. In the central narrative of life, this is the story we must strive to tell, to celebrate, and to champion.

Furthermore, in the waltz of life, self-care must become the rhythm, a drumbeat, a steadfast echo resonating in every corner of a Black woman's existence. Here are some strategies and tips to embed self-care within the daily cadence, nurturing mental health and emotional well-being:

- **Listening to the Inner Self:** Start by attuning to your body, your feelings, and your thoughts. This silent dialogue with your inner self is a compass guiding you to what your body and mind truly need. Listen to the whispers of fatigue, the sighs of stress, and the cries for rest. Responding to these signals with kindness and compassion forms the foundation of self-care.

- **Setting Boundaries:** Boundaries are the invisible lines that protect your peace. Set them in personal relationships, in professional engagements, and with yourself. Understand that *no* is a complete sentence. It is not a rejection of others, but an affirmation of self.

- **Prioritizing Rest:** Rest is a declaration of worthiness beyond productivity. It is the gentle embrace that allows rejuvenation. Schedule time for rest, be it in the form of sleep, leisure, or simply doing nothing. Rest is not a luxury; it is a right.

- **Movement and Nutrition:** Caring for the physical body directly impacts mental health. Engage in activities that make your body feel good, whether it's dancing, walking, or yoga. Nourish your body with food that fuels and pleases you. This is self-care in its most elemental form.

- **Creating Joy:** Identify activities that spark joy, then deliberately make time for them. Reading, painting, listening to music, or spending time in nature—these pockets of joy serve as antidotes to stress and fortify mental health.

- **Seeking Support:** Reach out to supportive communities, friends, or mental health professionals when needed. Asking for help is not a sign of weakness; it is an act of courage and self-care.

- **Mindful Practices:** Incorporate practices like mindfulness, meditation, or journaling. These tools anchor you to the present moment, nurture emotional well-being, and build resilience.

- **Cultivating Self-Compassion:** Recognize your own humanity. Accept that you will have days when you falter, when the world feels too heavy. Show yourself kindness in those moments, for self-compassion is the heart of self-care.

- **Affirmations:** Speak life into your existence through affirmations. Remind yourself of your worth, your strength, your resilience. Your words can be the balm to soothe wounds and the spark to light the way.

- **Celebrating Small Victories:** Often in the rush of life, we overlook the small victories, the tiny steps forward that signify growth. Perhaps you finished a book, had a positive conversation, took time for rest, or simply made it through the day. Celebrate these moments. Acknowledging and appreciating your progress, no matter how small, reinforces a positive mindset and serves as a reminder of your resilience and capability. It fuels self-confidence, boosts your mood, and strengthens your mental and emotional well-being. This practice of celebration is a powerful form of self-care, a beautiful dance of acknowledgment that intertwines with the rhythm of your life, coloring each day with a hue of joy and self-love.

The journey to prioritizing self-care is a path that meanders through fields of self-awareness, forests of resilience, and rivers of compassion. It asks of Black women to hold space for themselves, to honor their needs, to nurture their well-being amidst the cacophony of life. In this journey, self-care becomes not just an act, but a way of life, a symphony where every note is a testament to their strength, every rhythm an echo of their resilience, and every rest, a beautiful song of self-love.

In the majestic dance of life, time is the unseen conductor, tirelessly guiding the symphony of our days. Amidst the humdrum of responsibilities and the whirlwind of societal expectations, it often feels like we're caught in a relentless tempo, a never-ceasing rhythm that leaves little room for pause. However, for Black women who navigate a reality fraught with systemic challenges and disproportionate demands, carving out personal time and prioritizing rest becomes not just beneficial, but critically essential.

Imagine the rhythm of life as a complex composition, a symphony that crescendos with activity and softly decrescendos into silence with rest. If the music was always at its peak, its beauty would soon turn into cacophony, its harmony into disarray. Much like this symphony, our lives require a balance between action and rest, engagement and disengagement. The importance of personal time and rest lies in this balance.

Personal time is a sanctuary, a sacred space within the bustling landscape of life where Black women can honor their needs, nurture their spirit, and rejuvenate their energy. It's a harbor of quiet amidst the storm, a place to rest, reflect, and reconnect with their inner selves. Personal time provides an opportunity to recenter, to sift through thoughts and emotions, and to engage in activities that fuel joy and peace. It becomes an act of self-preservation, self-love, and, indeed, resistance against a world that often pushes for constant productivity at the expense of well-being.

Rest, on the other hand, is the silent healer, the unseen mender of the wear and tear of life. It is the soothing lullaby that invites restoration, the gentle tide that ebbs away stress and replenishes strength. Rest is a declaration of worth beyond productivity, an acknowledgment that one's value is inherent and not tied to constant output. For Black women, prioritizing rest becomes a profound statement that asserts their worthiness of care, relaxation, and peace, despite systemic narratives that suggest otherwise.

When personal time and rest become a priority, Black women are not merely surviving; they are thriving. They are asserting their right to balance, well-being, and peace. They are crafting a life that honors their needs and values their rest as much as their labor. They are, in essence, weaving a narrative that recognizes their humanity beyond societal roles and expectations, a narrative that celebrates their strength, resilience, and the courage to choose rest amidst the clamor of constant doing.

In the end, personal time and rest are not signs of luxury but symbols of necessity. They are not just desirable; they are vital. They are not just acts of self-care; they are acts of self-love. When Black women prioritize personal time and rest, they compose a symphony where the notes of self-care resonate as beautifully as the chords of hard work, where the harmony of rest echoes as powerfully as the melody of action. It is this symphony, rich in its complexity and profound in its beauty, that truly honors the resilience, strength, and holistic well-being of Black women.

In the splendid theater of life, boundaries are the unsung heroes, the invisible scripts that guard the stage of our existence. For Black women, who navigate a complex labyrinth of societal expectations and systemic pressures, setting and maintaining these boundaries become essential tools for self-preservation, critical lines in the sand that help them avoid the shadowy specter of burnout.

Burnout, the silent thief, creeps in with soft footsteps, robbing us of energy, enthusiasm, and ultimately, joy. It is the unwelcome guest at the banquet of life, consuming vitality and leaving in its wake a trail of fatigue, cynicism, and inefficacy. This drain of resources, both physical and emotional, becomes particularly challenging for Black women, who are often at the crossroads of intersectional oppressions and disproportionate demands, magnifying their risk of experiencing burnout.

Yet, in the face of this challenge, boundaries emerge as the stalwart protectors. They are the carefully drawn lines that delineate personal space, the shields that safeguard time, energy, and mental well-being. Boundaries allow Black women to assert their right to say 'no,' to prioritize their needs, and to disengage from situations that drain them.

Boundaries are more than mere markers; they are a profound declaration of self-respect and self-value. They communicate that a Black woman's time, energy, and emotional well-being are worth protecting. They broadcast to the world, and indeed to herself, that her needs matter, that she is not an endless resource to be drawn upon without respite.

In setting boundaries, Black women craft a protective sphere, within which their well-being is prioritized. They create buffer zones against overcommitment and overexertion, spaces where their peace is preserved, and their energy replenished. This act of setting boundaries is, therefore, a powerful form of self-care, a conscious decision to value personal well-being over societal expectations of constant giving.

Moreover, these boundaries also serve as models for others, setting a standard for how Black women expect to be treated and interacted with. They help redefine societal norms and expectations, championing a culture that respects and values Black women's needs, time, and energy.

Ultimately, boundaries are not walls shutting the world out; they are gateways ushering well-being in. They are not limitations, but liberations. They are not isolations, but the very elements that allow authentic, respectful connections.

Boundaries provide Black women with the freedom to engage with the world on their terms, enabling them to maintain their well-being and prevent burnout.

In the exquisite narrative of life, when Black women set and maintain boundaries, they are writing a story that echoes with respect for their well-being. They are creating a dance where every step protects their vitality, every twirl celebrates their needs, and every pause becomes a powerful *no* against burnout. It is this dance, this beautiful ballet of boundaries, that paves the path for a life where Black women's well-being is cherished, respected, and protected, a life that resonates with the harmonious melody of balance, respect, and self-care.

- **Communication:** Picture a quilt of clear skies. Here, the clouds of ambiguity have no place. In this landscape, Black women must articulate their needs and limits with clarity and conviction. Speak up about unmanageable workloads, or voice discomfort when personal space is invaded. Assertive, honest communication is a powerful tool to maintain one's boundaries.

- **Learn to Say No:** *No* is not a rejection, but a reclamation. It's a signal that one's well-being trumps the obligation to please. Much like a sturdy shield, it guards against undue burdens and keeps burnout at bay. Assert this right judiciously, choosing engagements that replenish rather than drain.

- **Prioritize Self-Care:** Envision self-care as a lush, verdant garden. Tend to it consistently. Whether it's regular exercise, a favorite hobby, or quiet time for reflection, prioritize activities that rejuvenate. This nurtured garden becomes a sanctuary from burnout.

- **Cultivate Mindfulness:** Mindfulness is the silent observer, the lighthouse guiding us to recognize signs of burnout. By staying present, Black women can detect when they're overextended or stressed and adjust their boundaries accordingly.

- **Delegate and Share Responsibilities:** Sometimes, the canvas of life brims with tasks that spread us too thin. Here, delegation emerges as an artist, freeing up space and time. By sharing tasks at home or delegating work assignments, Black women can ensure they're not shouldering disproportionate burdens.

- **Disengage from Toxicity:** In the elegant concert of life, dissonance disrupts harmony. Toxic relationships or environments can strain mental health, leading to burnout. It's important to disengage from such elements, creating boundaries that protect peace and well-being.

- **Invest in Rest:** Rest is the silent composer, crafting symphonies of renewal. It's an ally against burnout. Prioritize sufficient sleep, and incorporate breaks into daily routines. Rest is not wasted time, but a crucial investment in one's well-being.

- **Seek Support:** The journey of life, though individual, thrives on connection. Black women should not hesitate to seek support—be it professional, like therapists and counselors, or personal, like friends and family. These supportive networks can provide guidance and validation, and aid in boundary-setting.

- **Celebrate Autonomy:** Setting boundaries is an act of self-empowerment. Celebrate this autonomy. Each boundary set, each *no* pronounced, is a victory, a testament to the Black woman's agency and resilience. Cherish these triumphs.

In order to continue protecting our peace and nurturing our inner spirit, it's important for us to practice regular self-reflection. Self-reflection is the silent sentinel, the reflective mirror held up to the soul, revealing truths that the hustle of life often cloaks. Imagine it as a calm lake, undisturbed and serene, faithfully mirroring the world above. Black women, immersed in a sea of responsibilities and demands, would greatly benefit from regular introspective pauses by this metaphoric lake.

Self-reflection enables us to identify and understand our emotional states, pinpoint stressors, and assess the effectiveness of our boundaries. It acts as a barometer for our mental and emotional health, signaling when we may be veering toward the cliffs of burnout.

In the safe space of self-reflection, we can honestly ask ourselves: Are our boundaries serving us well? Are there areas in our lives where we feel overwhelmed or overburdened? Are we devoting enough time to self-care and rest? These insightful inquiries, carried out regularly, help us recognize when our boundaries need recalibration and reinforcement.

A strategy to facilitate self-reflection could be journaling. It's like crafting a personal biography, where thoughts, emotions, and experiences are the protagonists. The act of transferring thoughts onto paper provides clarity, revealing patterns and providing a deeper understanding of one's mental landscape.

Meditation can also serve as a vehicle for self-reflection, helping us tune into our inner world, making us more aware of our emotional states, and providing insights into our boundaries and their effectiveness.

In the grand interpretation of life, when Black women engage in regular self-reflection, they unlock a powerful tool for self-discovery and self-improvement. This strategy serves as a compass, guiding them away from the tumultuous seas of burnout and toward the tranquil shores of balance, wellness, and peace. By cultivating this practice, they not only reinforce their boundaries but also enrich their understanding of self, ultimately crafting a life that celebrates their well-being and resilience.

The art of setting boundaries and preventing burnout is akin to crafting a unique masterpiece. Each stroke of "no," each shade of self-care, each instance of delegation, shapes this work of art. The canvas might seem vast, the colors complex, but as Black women skillfully apply these techniques, they create a vibrant tableau that champions their well-being, a masterpiece that echoes with the melodies of balance, self-love, and resilience, warding off the shadows of burnout with the brilliant light of self-preservation.

In the magnificent symphony of existence, each note contributes to the harmonious whole. But what happens when one note, one pivotal note, is pressured to perform beyond its natural rhythm? The symphony risks discord. The critical note at risk? Black women, often shouldering weighty expectations and extensive responsibilities, both personal and professional, while neglecting the vital need for regular self-care.

Picture self-care as a lush oasis, a place of rejuvenation in the arid desert of relentless responsibilities. Neglect this oasis, and the desert can become overwhelming, often leading to burnout, stress, or health issues. Regular visits to this oasis, however, replenish and restore, enabling Black women to handle their external responsibilities with grace, energy, and resilience.

When Black women engage in regular self-care, they are not indulging in an optional luxury; they are investing in a mandatory resource. The act of self-care is a bold proclamation of self-worth. It signals the recognition of one's inherent value and the understanding that, to nurture others, one must first nurture oneself. It is in this self-nourishing space that Black women replenish their physical, emotional, and mental reserves, equipping them to effectively manage their myriad roles and responsibilities.

Self-care takes many forms. It might be a morning ritual of meditation, creating a serene space for mental clarity amidst a day teeming with demands. It could be a regular exercise routine, fortifying physical strength to tackle the challenges of the day. It might manifest in boundaries set around work and personal life, ensuring that rest and rejuvenation balance out the weight of responsibility.

It could even be as simple as pursuing a beloved hobby, offering an emotional breather in a sea of tasks.

By regularly retreating to this self-care oasis, Black women cultivate the strength, resilience, and balance needed to navigate their external responsibilities. They equip themselves with the tools necessary to respond to life's demands effectively, without depleting their reserves. Moreover, the practice of self-care fosters increased productivity, enhanced self-esteem, and improved mental health—factors that positively influence their capacity to manage external responsibilities.

Importantly, regular self-care sends a powerful message to the world: Black women are not only givers, but also receivers. They are not perpetually strong towers who stand unbending against the winds of responsibility, but complex beings who need and deserve nurturing. This understanding helps dismantle the harmful stereotypes often associated with Black women, fostering a healthier societal perception.

In the grand symphony of life, regular self-care ensures that the note of Black women resonates clearly, richly, and strongly. By consistently visiting the oasis of self-care, they honor themselves and their needs, fortifying their capacity to meet external responsibilities. In doing so, they create a melody of balance, well-being, and resilience that not only enriches their lives, but also contributes harmoniously to the symphony of existence. As they embody this powerful truth, the world must listen, learn, and reorient toward a more compassionate understanding of Black women's strength, one that celebrates their vulnerability, resilience, and innate worth.

In the beautiful tapestry of existence, each strand, each thread has its unique hue, its distinct texture. Every individual thread contributes to the rich design, bringing vibrancy and depth. Black women are such threads—radiant and vital, essential in creating the beautiful tableau of humanity. To fully appreciate the tapestry, each thread must acknowledge its beauty, embrace its worth.

Consider for a moment a garden, abundant in diversity, flourishing with unique and exotic flowers. Black women are the rare orchids, the midnight roses, the vibrant hibiscus. Their physical beauty is like the mesmerizing colors and forms of these flowers, striking and varied. In a world often governed by a narrow definition of beauty, it is crucial that Black women celebrate their physical diversity, their unique patterns and shades. Embracing their physical beauty is not merely an act of vanity; it is a bold affirmation of their identity, a powerful assertion of their place in the world's garden.

When Black women acknowledge their worth, they recognize the invaluable qualities they bring to society. Their strength, resilience, compassion, intelligence, creativity, and countless other attributes make them vital contributors to their communities and the world. By acknowledging their worth, they reject the marginalizing narratives and biases that seek to undermine them, empowering themselves and inspiring others.

Embracing physical beauty and acknowledging worth have far-reaching effects on Black women's mental health, self-esteem, and overall well-being. They combat the harmful effects of societal prejudice, racism, and sexism, reinforcing positive self-perception and fostering mental resilience. This process contributes to the holistic development of Black women, positively impacting their relationships, careers, and personal growth.

Beyond the individual, the acknowledgment of Black women's beauty and worth is a collective necessity. It challenges and expands society's rigid beauty norms, fostering greater acceptance and diversity. It raises the visibility of Black women in various societal spheres, promoting inclusivity and equality. It educates future generations, modeling for young Black girls that they are beautiful, they are valuable, and they have every right to fully occupy their space in the world.

Much like a river that knows its course, flowing unapologetically, carving its path, Black women who embrace their beauty and worth chart a powerful course for themselves. They become a beacon of strength, a testament to resilience, a celebration of diversity, and a symbol of pride. As they stand tall like the baobab tree in the African savannah, their roots deep, their branches spread wide, they proclaim to the world their innate beauty, their inherent worth.

In the vivid mosaic of humanity, when Black women embrace their physical beauty and acknowledge their worth, the design becomes richer, the colors deeper, and the patterns more intricate. They weave their vibrant threads into the fabric of society, creating a more inclusive, equitable, and beautiful world. It is a world that celebrates the unique beauty and extraordinary worth of every individual, a world where the tapestry of humanity is indeed grand, and the garden of life is genuinely diverse and vibrant.

journaling questions

1. How do you perceive the interconnectedness of your physical and mental health, and how do you prioritize each in your daily routines?

2. In moments of introspection, how do you balance your self-worth with your professional achievements? What steps can you take to ensure you prioritize your well-being above accolades?

3. How do you currently allocate time for personal rest and rejuvenation? Are there moments when you feel guilty for taking this time, and how can you transform this guilt into affirmation?

4. Reflect on a time when you felt on the brink of burnout. What boundaries could have been set to prevent reaching that point, and how can you implement them moving forward?

5. How has prioritizing self-care benefited your ability to handle external responsibilities? Are there areas of self-care you've overlooked that could further enhance your capacity to manage obligations?

6. How do you currently celebrate your physical beauty? Are there societal narratives or personal beliefs that sometimes challenge this celebration, and how can you work to transform or reject them?

7. How do you affirm your inherent worth, separate from any external factors or achievements? What practices or rituals help reinforce this acknowledgment?

8. How do you navigate the tightrope of ambition and self-care? Are there any compromises you've made that you regret, or any boundaries you're proud of setting?

9. Reflect on the external pressures that might affect your perception of beauty, success, and worth. How can you work to internalize a self-affirming narrative instead?

10. How does your community or social circle support or challenge your self-care practices? Are there conversations you can initiate or boundaries you can set to enhance communal support for individual well-being?

affirmations

1. My physical and mental well-being are paramount. I honor my body and mind, nourishing them with love and care.

2. While I am proud of my achievements, I prioritize my well-being above all. My worth is intrinsic and not solely defined by my professional successes.

3. I cherish and protect my personal time, knowing that rest and rejuvenation are essential for my holistic health.

4. I set firm boundaries to protect my energy and space, ensuring that I do not stretch myself to the point of burnout.

5. By caring for myself, I equip myself with the strength and resilience to handle my external responsibilities with grace.

6. I embrace and celebrate my unique physical beauty, understanding that I am a reflection of generations of strength and resilience.

7. I am worthy, valuable, and deserving of love, respect, and care, regardless of external validation.

8. Every moment I spend on self-care is an investment in my well-being and future. I am intentional with how I allocate my time.

9. Rest is not a luxury; it's a necessity. I give myself permission to pause and rejuvenate whenever I need to.

10. I celebrate every part of who I am—my strengths, vulnerabilities, achievements, and learnings. I am a holistic being deserving of holistic care.

Chapter 6

the influence of societal constructs and personal experiences on perception of beauty

"You can't eat beauty, it doesn't feed you...
beauty was not a thing that I could acquire or
consume, it was something that I just had to be.
You can't rely on how you look to sustain yourself.
What actually sustains us, what is fundamentally
beautiful, is compassion—for yourself and for those
around you. That kind of beauty inflames the
heart and enchants the soul."

—Lupita Nyong'o

Have you ever had a Black baby doll? Did you want one? Not me! As a child, I idolized Barbie's perfectly laid blonde tendrils that flowed down to the middle of her back. In contrast to my daily life, there was one figure that seemed to have it all: Barbie. This blonde doll with her perfectly styled hair became my alter ego, embodying everything I longed for but couldn't attain. My Jamaican parents didn't believe in allowances in exchange for chores. Chores were the job of children to "earn their keep." So, growing up in our small terrace house in southeast London, I didn't have any illusions about being in the lap of luxury and living in a dream house with a pool, like Barbie did. My parents only bought dolls at Christmas. Barbie was always at the top of my list. The fact that I was so enamored by her even though she looked nothing like me was an inconvenience I had learned to overlook. None of my friends or cousins had Black baby dolls either, so I wasn't alone.

The only semblance of what was supposed to be a Black baby doll I had ever seen for sale was called a golliwog. Golliwogs were sold in many convenience stores all across South London. And I hated them. They scared me with their black skin, huge white eyes, and clownlike, oversized red lips. My skin was a warm brown, my eyes a soft black, and my lips, while full, were not exaggerated like a clown's. So, why was a toy that looked so dissimilar to me being sold as something I would enjoy? My five-year-old self was confused. I wondered where this doll had come from. Wherever it was from, I wished it would go back there, never to return. Its very existence repelled my tiny body, even though at the time I didn't understand why.

I would later discover that Florence Kate Upton, a cartoonist, created the frightful figure known as a golliwog (or golliwogg, or even just golly) in the late nineteenth century. It was designed to be a type of rag doll and found popularity in various parts of the world, despite being clearly rooted in blackface minstrel tradition. It appeared in children's books in the late nineteenth century, usually depicted as a type of rag doll. It was reproduced, both by commercial and hobby toymakers, as a children's soft toy called the "golliwog" and had great popularity in the Southern United States, the UK, South Africa, and Australia into the 1970s. The doll is characterized by jet black skin, eyes rimmed in white, exaggerated red lips, and frizzy hair, based on the blackface minstrel tradition. Since the twentieth century, the word has been considered a racial slur against Black people.[80]

Of course that had happened to me—yet another reason to hate the golliwog! The first time, I was bewildered, scared, and sad. I was playing with a group of my friends in the playground of our South London primary school. Our games of choice were typically jacks, hopscotch, Cat's Cradle, and marbles. That was more than enough to keep us busy, along with the occasional game of Kiss Chase, which was one of my personal favorites. But the one day I remember, the game took a turn for the worse. The boys were chasing me and my group of friends. We were the five-year-old children of immigrants from all over the world—Jamaica, Africa, Sri Lanka, and Pakistan. But they weren't chasing us to give us a peck on the cheek when they caught us. They were chasing us and calling us golliwogs. We ran screaming. This game was not fun. I was horrified. Later, I remember thinking about what had happened and asking myself questions to try to understand. Did they think we looked like golliwogs? I knew we didn't. So, why had they said that? My young mind imagined what had happened and replayed it over and over again, trying to find meaning. I couldn't.

Contrasting the disturbing appearance of the golliwog, Barbie—with her slender body, full breasts, small hips, and dainty hands and feet—appealed to my aesthetic sense. Her physical attributes embodied the beauty standard I found myself drawn to, a standard far removed from the racialized caricature the golliwog represented. Her teeth were perfectly white, with a cute pointy nose and thin pink lips—not big, red, and obnoxious ones like that awful Black

---

80 Pilgrim, David. 2000. "The Golliwog Caricature: Anti-Black Imagery at the Jim Crow Museum." Jim Crow Museum. jimcrowmuseum.ferris.edu/golliwog/homepage.htm.

doll. My cousin had one, and I was deathly afraid of it. Its face angered me, even though I wasn't sure why.

Barbie, on the other hand, made me feel happy. Her world of endless possibilities and beautiful clothes filled me with delight, a stark contrast to the fear I felt toward the golliwog. She had multiple changes of clothes and shoes, the dream house, and, of course, Ken, the perfect boyfriend. I loved her. And I wanted her to love me back. So I took care of her by changing her outfits and driving her across the living room floor in her pink car. She had places to go and people to see. Her days were full of shopping sprees and parties with cool friends. I meticulously brushed her hair for date night, adorning it with a little clip that matched her dress and tiny heels.

I wanted my coily kinks to be mid-back as well, but...shrinkage. I begged my mother constantly to straighten my hair. But she ignored my pleas, and only agreed on special occasions like Christmas and my birthday. I was five the first time my mom straightened my hair with a metal hot comb. I distinctly remember the sizzle as it was wrapped into a damp cloth on the kitchen counter after being heated on the small gas stove in our tiny kitchen. The warmth on the back of my neck intensified my fear of being burned as she slowly and meticulously pulled the comb through my resistant curls. The unforgiving, tightly aligned teeth of the comb gnawed at the roots near my scalp, releasing a sigh when my hair finally relinquished its willful disobedience. It relaxed because there was no fighting this. It was finally happening.

As scared as I was of the hot steam, I wanted this more than anything else at that moment. Narrow shoulders raised, I flinched at each hot breath on the back of my neck. But I dared not make a sound. My mother had already warned me that jumping could mean a burn. She also had little patience for little hands attempting to feel the progress she was making. A quick rap on the knuckles with her comb sent my hands right back into my lap. I willed myself to just relax, and I twirled my fingers around each other. I wiggled my toes gently. I thought about how I would feel when I was finally allowed to gaze into the mirror to witness the miraculous transformation. I would do anything to take my mind off this hour of pain because it would bring me at least a week of pleasure.

When my mother finally laid down her tools, my previously stubborn coils had surrendered to the heat. In place of the familiar tight curls, a sleek, straight curtain of hair flowed down my back. It wasn't quite mid-back length, but that was okay. I still dashed as fast as I could to see myself in the mirror. "I love my hair!" Swinging my slick hair around my shoulders was such a welcome reprieve from the thick braids tied with ribbons I usually wore on each side of my head. This was what I wanted every day, but my mother warned me again before I could even open my mouth to ask. She only agreed to the arduous process for special engagements. I would have to be satisfied with that, or nothing at all.

The week of pleasure would be cut short in its tracks if I ran too much on the playground to get it all messy and sweaty. It meant I couldn't get it wet in the bath, which meant no playing with toys and splashing with my siblings. My mother gave me an extra-large silk scarf to wear from her priceless nightstand, which also contained other treasures like pantyhose and bras that I was too young to wear but wanted to touch just to experience how they felt against my palm. Instead, I would need to be content with running my fingers back and forth across the knot in the scarf to ensure it was secure for the night. I would need my newly straightened hair to be protected from my very worn, moisture-depriving cotton pillowcase.

As the years rolled on, the process of managing my hair evolved. Entering adulthood, my hair routine took on a more potent edge—every few weeks I repeated the process with chemical relaxers, each time with a fresh fear of painful chemical burns on my scalp, making my heart race. But as soon as I entered college, I began the ritual of relaxing my hair. When I was a teenager, my mother was adamant about me not getting a chemical relaxer. She had instead opted for the kinder, gentler Jheri Curl, an alternative that unfortunately made me the object of jokes during high school and middle school. Bottles of activator needed to be kept on hand to keep my curls nice and moist. My classmates called it "Jheri Curl Juice." But I ignored that. I had to be sure not to rest my hair on any surface for too long. A greasy headprint would indicate I had been there. How embarrassing! And besides, I often reminded my classmates that this was actually a "Leisure Curl," not the obnoxious Jheri Curl. This Wave Nouveau was much looser in curl pattern than the coiffed afro worn by the likes of "gangster rappers" such as Straight Outta Compton's NWA. I was trying to emulate the refined, professional women I saw in magazines, not portray the image of a West Coast Gang Banger, as the Jheri Curl was often stereotyped. Couldn't they understand that?

And since my mother didn't approve of my "ladylike" obsession with needing straight hair, I waited until I entered college to go from curly to straight. I scraped together any money I could save to get my hair done every six weeks. Most of us couldn't afford top-shelf relaxers like Mizani, so we opted for the cheapest brand, called Bantu. It was notoriously strong, and the horror stories of scabs on scalps were enough evidence for us that it worked exactly as it was supposed to. That new growth needed to be bone-straight, just like the rest of our hair! In the days leading up to my appointment, my friends had warned me against scratching my scalp. Doing so could be detrimental because it left the pores of the scalp vulnerable to the white, strong, pungent chemicals that were slathered on the unruly new growth. But none of that could happen unless you could sit through thirty minutes of your scalp feeling like it was on fire, no matter how much petroleum gel had been used to protect it. When the hairdresser at the salon asked if it was burning, we dared not say yes for fear that she would wash out the chemicals too soon. That meant we would waste the forty dollars it cost to undergo this arduous process. The thought was unbearable! With burning eyes and a burning scalp, I tapped my toes on the salon floor, attempting to distract myself from the pain. But we waited and counted down the time until those thirty minutes were up. There was a sigh of relief as cool water touched our tortured scalps. There was a small smile as we felt gentle fingers and shampoo scrubbing the chemicals from our new growth. It was no match for Bantu! It had melted away to meet the relaxed hair that we willed to grow to that coveted mid-back length.

To ensure I had enough coins for my beauty routine and fashion needs, I resorted to a diet of Ramen noodles and three-dollar pizzas from the local pizza place. This allowed me to get my hair done, my nails filled with acrylic, my toes pedicured, and even buy a budget-busting outfit from Forever 21 at the only mall near the University of Florida campus. I was ready for the weekend! Fraternity parties were our main outlet for fun. So, outfits and shoes were selected and laid on the bed hours ahead of time. Cute skirts, tiny midriff tops, and stiletto heels were modeled, so we could vote on a group consensus of the vibe for the night. It was going to be a long one as well!

An hour before it was time to strut across campus, my roommates and I jostled for position in front of the mirror to plaster on lipstick and black eyeliner, wondering how it was possible that we had all been color matched for NC45 at the mall's MAC counter despite our various skin tones of caramel, copper, bronze, and mocha. Fashion Fair was too heavy and caked our faces like smiling masks. Maybelline and CoverGirl makeup never had colors that matched either. So, NC45 for all it was!

Nonetheless, the final step was placing the multiple curling irons we had all collected on the dorm room desk and plugging them into the surge protector. Some were ceramic. Others were gold-plated. Some could crimp. And of course, we had at least one flat iron among the various barrel sizes. The one common denominator was that they could all get our hair bone-straight. We carefully applied Ampro Pro Styl Marcel Wax. That was a must-have and definitely not to be skimped on. Baby hairs needed to be laid to the Gods. Let's Jam Edge Control Gel made that wish come true and was not to be spared either. We slathered it on and meticulously shaped our curls, adhering them to our foreheads and sculpting them like artists with our worn toothbrushes set aside specifically for this task.

Given the steamy atmosphere of the gym, a common venue for frat parties, our hairstyles needed to be resilient. We knew the heat and humidity would put our carefully crafted looks to the test. Our five-dollar entrance fee was hard-earned from our Ramen noodle diets. And for our troubles, we would dance with wild abandon to the sweet sounds of 2 Live Crew, 69 Boyz, and Sir Mix-A-Lot. The beat dropped and bass rattled the windows as we forgot for a moment all of the preparation we had put into our ladylike appearance that didn't quite match our gyrating hips, dancing in the dark. "Baby got back," we chanted as we looked back at it.

We scattered outside in embarrassment when the last song came to an end, and we saw faces that matched the sweaty bodies we had been grinding against all night. The overhead fluorescent lights brought us back to the reality of the dingy gym. We erupted into laughter, playfully pointing at the state of each other's hair, our faces caught in the harsh, unforgiving fluorescence, glistening like morning dew. Despite our meticulous preparation, we always stumbled outside with fluffy halos of hair billowing like crowns of dandelion wishes coming true around our heads. We marched defiantly into the cool night air, back to the dorms, with our heels clutched in our damp palms. This process would be repeated every weekend—the battle against our hair. Our hair always won. It was undefeated.

Reflecting on these memories now brings to mind a question I was asked on a podcast a few months ago—a question that left me speechless and a little sad. The host asked a panel of Black women who work in social justice and advocacy when the last time was that we felt truly beautiful. The question, I believe, left us all in a state of shock. It was something I had never really thought about before, much less been asked about. Though I had always understood, on an intellectual level, the sentiment that "Black is Beautiful," I found myself struggling to provide an easy, straightforward answer to this question. But as I searched my memory and waited for the other panelists to respond, I started to feel a sinking feeling in the pit of my stomach. One by one, each of us admitted we couldn't think of a particular time. Ever. I answered honestly as well. "I don't know. I can't think of a time that I remember."

According to historians at the Smithsonian's National Museum of African American History and Culture, toys offer opportunities to reiterate children's inclusion or "otherness" in a society that has traditionally viewed Blacks as second-class citizens. Prior to the 1950s, dolls that were anthropologically correct in their depiction of African Americans were nonexistent or not widely marketed. The media, including the toy industry, was rife with negative, exaggerated depictions of Black individuals—caricatures that emphasized stereotypes and minimized our beauty.

These depictions deemphasized the beauty and humanity of Black people. Understanding the cultural, social, and practical significance of dolls, it is important to consider how a lack of positive representation can have an adverse impact on children's self-esteem, confidence, and perception. Through dolls, children can learn about their self-worth and roles within society, as confirmed in the Clark study of Black children's racial perceptions. The Clarks' Supreme Court testimony contributed to the outcome of the *Brown v. Board of Education of Topeka* case, which led to the desegregation of American schools.[81]

In the 1940s, psychologists Kenneth and Mamie Clark designed and conducted a series of experiments known colloquially as "the doll tests" to study the psychological effects of segregation on African American children.

The Clarks used four dolls, identical except for color, to test children's racial perceptions. Their subjects, Black children between the ages of three and seven,

81 Dixon, Alexis, and Elaine Nichols. n.d. "Dolls Hold Significance and Break Cultural and Racial Barriers." National Museum of African American History and Culture. nmaahc.si.edu/explore/stories/dolls-hold-significance-and-break-cultural-and-racial-barriers.

were asked a series of questions and asked to identify both the race of the dolls and which color doll they preferred. They asked the children to choose between a white doll and—because, at the time, no brown dolls were available—a white doll painted brown. The children overwhelmingly preferred the white doll and assigned positive characteristics to it. From their research, the Clarks concluded that the effects of prejudice, discrimination, and segregation were insidious, creating feelings of inferiority among African American children and causing profound damage to their self-esteem.[82]

Later researchers hypothesized and tested the significant impact of children not seeing positive images that look like them to determine whether Black children also have a bias toward whiteness. In 2010, renowned child psychologist Margaret Beale Spencer, a leading voice in the field of child development and a professor at the University of Chicago, was brought on board as a consultant by CNN. Her expertise proved invaluable. . Spencer's test aimed to recreate the landmark Doll Test from the 1940s, conducted by the Clarks.

In the new study, Spencer's researchers asked the younger children a series of questions and had them answer by pointing to one of five cartoon pictures that varied in skin color from light to dark. The older children were asked the same questions using the same cartoon pictures, and were then asked a series of questions about a color bar chart that showed light to dark skin tones.

The tests unveiled a stark truth: white children, as a whole, showed a high degree of what researchers call "white bias." They associated the color of their own skin with positive attributes and darker skin tones with negative ones, highlighting the pervasive nature of racial biases in our society. Spencer said even Black children, as a whole, have some bias toward whiteness, but far less than white children.[83]

82   "Brown v. Board: The Significance of the 'Doll Test.' " 2023. Legal Defense Fund. www.naacpldf.
      org/brown-vs-board/significance-doll-test/.

83   Billante, Jill, and Chuck Hadad. 2010. "Study: White and black children biased toward lighter skin."
      CNN. www.cnn.com/2010/US/05/13/doll.study/index.html.

Even if we don't fully understand what is happening around us, our brains process stimuli. When these stimuli don't align with our self-image, it affects how we think about ourselves and our place in the world. It can have a profound effect on your identity at your very core, in the deepest recesses you didn't even think existed. Not seeing ourselves reflected in the environments we inhabit leads to a disconnect from our existence, which creates an otherworldly experience, like being a stranger in town. We are always on the outskirts of conversations and societal relationships outside of our friends and loved ones, without the ability to catch up because to do so would take too long. The task appears insurmountable and evolves into a lifelong challenge that begins with the physical but, in its impact, affects the mental so much more.

The same homogenous archetypes of beauty, typically favoring Eurocentric features, have dominated the narrative of how Blackness is perceived within this construct. Black women have often been stereotyped as less attractive, less desirable, and less worthwhile in society's hierarchy of beauty. In this system, the closer one's physical features are to the construct of whiteness, the higher their perceived beauty. Conversely, Blackness has been unjustly placed at the bottom of this ladder, devalued, and dismissed. Blackness, seen as an invalid construct, is often placed at the very bottom of this beauty hierarchy, as if we've not even stepped onto the ladder's first rung, its top disappearing into the stormy clouds above.

For American women of African ancestry, the enduring scars of American slavery add a complex layer to the societal burdens they bear, from systemic racism to economic inequities. Mainstream beauty industries have traditionally marginalized Black women's attributes, often branding them as masculine or undesirable. For example, curvy body types and fuller lips, common among many Black women, were long overlooked until popularized by predominantly white celebrities, reflecting how European aesthetics are often considered the standard of beauty in America.[84] Even within the Black community, a bias toward lighter complexions can yield societal advantages. For instance, studies have shown that individuals with lighter skin often attain higher levels of educational and occupational success.[85] Black women's hair is policed: Looser curls and straightened hair are celebrated,[86] whereas afros and traditionally Black hairstyles have resulted in academic and professional dismissals.

DC blogger Cashawn Thompson launched the empowering hashtag #BlackGirlMagic in response to a problematic *Psychology Today* article, sparking a nationwide movement that celebrates and affirms Black women's beauty and achievements. The hashtag ignited a nationwide empowerment movement, providing a platform for the celebration and recognition of Black women's achievements. It served as an uplifting counter-narrative to mainstream depictions, affirming the beauty of Black women in a world that often fails to do so.

An article from the *International Journal of Women's Dermatology* discusses research into the #BlackGirlMagic movement. The study investigates the movement's impact on Black women's self-esteem. A survey was administered to 134 young Black women on Instagram. The majority of participants identified as having Fitzpatrick skin types IV or V and/or classified their hair texture type as 4C or 4B (kinky/coily curls).

Users were asked about the perceived impact of the hashtag on their self-esteem. 82 percent of participants reported experiencing discrimination because of their race. Many participants reported at one point wishing that they did not have features attributable to their race: 78 percent had thought this about their hair texture,

84   Banks, Ingrid. *Hair Matters: Beauty, Power, and Black Women's Consciousness.* New York: NYU Press, 2000.

85   Ryabov, Igor. "How much does physical attractiveness matter for blacks? Linking skin color, physical attractiveness, and black status attainment." *Race and Social Problems* 11, no. 1 (2019): 68–79.

86   Craig, Maxine Leeds. *Ain't I a beauty queen?: Black women, beauty, and the politics of race.* Oxford University Press, 2002.

64 percent about their skin complexion, and 60 percent about their facial features (wishes for smaller lips and noses were a resounding response to this question). In addition, 82 percent believed that the #BlackGirlMagic social media movement had had an impact on their self-esteem, with 69 percent of those participants reporting improved self-esteem after hashtag interaction.

Psychology studies have confirmed the association between the internalization of social media beauty standards and unhappiness with one's appearance.[87] Understanding the depth of this issue requires us to delve into its roots, complex as they may be. Unpacking the origins of these harmful beauty standards is crucial, as they deeply affect self-acceptance and self-esteem. It strikes at the heart of the ancestral cultural importance of notions of beauty and what they mean in relation to healthy self-acceptance and a correspondingly high level of self-esteem. First, we need to understand the origin of the false narrative: a lack of desirability. This narrative has distorted a rich history of reverence for attractiveness within the African diaspora.

The philosophy of beauty is an evolving discourse in African philosophy. This does not imply that there was no African conception of beauty. Rather, African philosophers are now beginning to earnestly have more than a passing and non-technical interest in the reality of the beautiful. In the context of African cultures, the concept of beauty is indeed unique. In many African cultures, beauty is often closely associated with femininity. Some of the male participants in a sociological field study by Arden Haselmann in Senegal associated beauty with women. African conceptualizations of beauty are in feminine terms, and perhaps every usage of the word "beauty" or "beautiful" is usually constructed to celebrate womanhood or feminine spirit.[88]

87 Fardouly, Jasmine, Phillippa C. Diedrichs, Lenny R. Vartanian, and Emma Halliwell. "Social comparisons on social media: The impact of Facebook on young women's body image concerns and mood." *Body Image* 13 (2015): 38–45.

88 Haselmann, Arden. 2014. " 'All Women Talk'—A Study of Beauty and Female Identity in Senegalese Culture." *Independent Study Project (ISP) Collection.*

In Africa, beauty connotes a celebration of worth, value, and quality; it's not just about physical attractiveness, but also the essence of a person's character and their societal contributions. Hence, the concept of beauty in Africa is quite broad and varies from one cultural community to another. However, as Vimbai Matiza rightly observes, the concept of beauty in Africa tends to speak of the external and internal qualities of a person or object. Moreover, the concept of beauty in Africa bears some moral intonations beyond *teleos*, which historians identify as the ancient Greek term for an end, fulfillment, completion, goal, or aim.

For example, Matiza notes that in the language of Shona in Zimbabwe, the word *kunaka* (beauty) denotes well-groomed character and physical attractiveness. In Annang of Nigeria, the word *ntuen-akpo* is used metaphorically to refer to a woman who only has physical attractiveness, but lacks good manners. *Ntuen-akpo* is a type of attractive pepper that can hurt the tongue when tasted or eaten. A woman described as *ntuen-akpo* might find that despite her physical attractiveness, her lack of good manners may hinder her from being fully valued or desired in her community.

Another defining characteristic of beauty in African philosophy is its functional aspect—beauty is not merely aesthetic but also has a role to play in society. Matiza confirms that in an African context, "beauty is not for the sake of being beautiful." According to him, beauty has a social character; rather than being individualistic, it is communal. Matiza argues that "from an African perspective, the concept of beauty has to have a purpose, which it fulfills."[89] Beauty must serve to communicate values, norms, morals, and purpose. Beauty must edify the community.

---

89   Matiza, Vimbai. 2013. "African Social Concept of Beauty: Its Relevancy to Literary Criticism." *Asian Journal of Social Science & Humanities* 2 (2): 61.

In his research on Sudanese beauty concepts, Baqie Muhammad concluded that "beauty encompasses 'good behavior, skills, knowledge, and dress, in addition to physical features.' "[90] There cannot be beauty for its own sake; beauty must be intended to serve society.

Matiza argues that the notion of beauty cannot center solely on the individual. Without considering its effects on the community, it is un-African in nature. He maintains that beauty in an African context implies working together. In other words, beauty must be a reflection of the interconnectedness that characterizes African societies. It's not just about individual aesthetics, but also about contributing positively to the community.[91]

Polycarp Ikuenobe argues that in African societies, the measure of beauty—whether it be in a person or an object—is how much it improves harmony and order within the community. The beauty of a person or thing should be participatory and interconnected rather than individualistic, and it should be meaningful only in the context of the acceptable standards of the community. Ikuenobe notes that if a person's action is seen as "fostering or leading to disharmony in nature, community, and reality, then it is considered bad or ugly."[92]

The Ubuntu dictum states: I am because we are. What this means is that a person's beauty should communicate universality. To this extent, the concept of beauty in Africa is objective in that it communicates a communal standard, but it is also subjective in that the standard of beauty is different from community to community. I am beautiful because my community members affirm my beauty as such, but outside my community, the affirmed

90   Muhammad, Baqie. 1993. "The Sudanese Concept of Beauty, Spirit Possession, and Power." *Folklore Forum* 26 (1/2): 43–67.

91   Matiza, 2013.

92   Ikuenobe, Polycarp. 2016. "Good and Beautiful: A Moral-Aesthetic View of Personhood in African Communal Traditions." *Essays in Philosophy* 17 (1): 125–163.

beauty may be disavowed. What is considered beautiful is meaningful only to the people in that context.

The general concept for Afrocentric relational theory is "I am because we are." This means people, objects, phenomena, and concepts do not exist alone, individuated, or isolated. Rather, they exist in relation to other people, objects, phenomena, and concepts. An Igbo proverb articulates this notion as *Ife kwulu, ife akwudebeya*, suggesting that no entity exists in isolation—when one thing stands, another stands alongside it, emphasizing interconnectedness.[93]

Through this historically accurate lens, we can see that the stereotypical defeminization and further intentional masculinization of Black women is not an inherently ancestral practice, philosophy, or belief in the precolonial African diaspora. In African ancestral tradition, being a Black woman, being feminine, and being beautiful were considered positive qualities, especially when combined with qualities like strength, wisdom, or compassion. However, this standard of beauty was designed within the community, agreed upon therein, and varied greatly from community to community. And in terms of the views of outsiders in precolonial Africa, we see a very familiar construct, more similar to what we know of the stereotypes and archetypes we observe in contemporary Western culture that have proliferated since colonization both here and around the globe, even back to the African continent itself, in the "othering" depiction of Black bodies and Black beauty.

Sociology Professor Tom Meisenhelder from California State University points out that influential early discourse about the African other within the European cultural repertoire relied heavily on the writings of the ancient Greeks. These writings usually took the form of supposed travelers' tales

93   Ibanga, Diana-Abasi. 2017. "The Concept of Beauty in African Philosophy." *Africology: The Journal of Pan African Studies* 10, no. 7 (September): 249–260.

about Africa and Africans, as well as the writings of philosophers and poets. There can be no doubt that both of these forms are premised on the idea that Europe or Greece is at the center of the important world and Africa is a marginal and alien place. As a result, the Greek image of the African other stressed its strangeness relative to the familiarity of other "Europeans."[94]

However, since the time of the eighth-century-BCE Greek poet Homer, Greek descriptions have also included a more positive image of the African. The more positive images of Africans described Africa as a place very near the sun and especially dear to the gods. Greek descriptions of Africa include tales of human beings of great physical and cultural beauty.[95]

Contemporary Nigerian-Finnish and Swedish author and social critic Minna Salami confirms Snowden's research, conducted in 1970, with her recent assertion that Western history is also sprinkled with appreciation of the beauty of African women, particularly dark-skinned African women. There has always been a simultaneous awe of Black women's ethereal beauty. In fact, in some of the oldest representations of African womanhood in the West—black at the time being the color of divinity, earth, and fertility—women of dark hue from the ancient kingdoms such as Küsh, Meroë, and Nubia, were valued as especially beautiful and feminine.

Favorable depictions of Black beauty can also be found in remnants of European culture, such as the Black Queen of Sheba portrayed at the monastery of Klosterneuburg in Austria, the Black Venus, or the shield of Kirchberg, which portrays a female Black deity holding a lily stalk. In the Historiated Bible in Dresden, Moses begs an African femme fatale to be his wife "in the Land of the Blacks." Similarly, the Krumlov Compilation in Prague depicts the Black Bride of the Song of Songs, a gracious, elegant African woman who in the Bible says, "I am Black, but comely, O ye daughters of Jerusalem, as the tents of Kedar, as the curtains of Solomon."

---

94 Meisenhelder, Tom. 2003. "African Bodies: 'Othering' the African in Precolonial Europe." *Race, Gender & Class* 10 (3): 101.

95 Snowden, Frank M. *Blacks in Antiquity*. Cambridge: Harvard University Press, 1970.

According to Salami, the Western world has for a long time tried to distort and demonize African womanhood. From depictions in historical art to the portrayal of modern-day icons like Serena Williams, it's clear that the campaign to demean Black beauty is not only ongoing, but also far-reaching. [96]

Historically, narratives that undermine African womanhood have not always been intentionally destructive, but their outcomes often have been. The notion of dehumanizing Africans, particularly women of the African diaspora, was cultivated post-colonization. This is even more troubling given the fact that Blackness as a construct itself is relatively new in the history of the world and has no biological basis. Rather, it serves to weaponize racist philosophy with no scientific foundation to create a social hierarchy that marginalizes, excludes, and ultimately intends to destroy. The tools of unfamiliarity, folklore, and certain interpretations of Christian doctrine were weaponized in this dehumanization. And as we know, dehumanization in this sense requires indoctrination. The result is a degradation of not only the body, but also the mind and the soul.

Given the US's history and ongoing struggle with racism, African American women confront numerous identity and beauty issues, from societal beauty standards to underrepresentation in the media. Since 1619, African American women and their beauty have been juxtaposed against White beauty standards, particularly pertaining to their skin color and hair. During slavery, Black women who were lighter-skinned and had features that were associated with mixed progeny (e.g., wavy or straight hair, white or European facial features) tended to be house slaves and those Black women with darker skin hues, kinky hair, and broader facial features tended to be field slaves.[97]

---

96 Salami, Minna. 2015. "A brief history of portrayals of African women in the west | Feminism and Social Criticism by Minna Salami." MsAfropolitan. msafropolitan.com/2015/07/a-brief-history-of-portrayals-of-african-women-in-the-west.html.

97 Owens Patton, Tracey. 2006. "Hey Girl, Am I More Than My Hair?: African American Women and Their Struggles with Beauty, Body Image, and Hair." NWSA Journal 18, no. 2 (Summer): 26–27.

The beauty standard that values whiteness over the various hues of melanin was established during precolonial and colonial times, perpetuated during slavery, and persists even after Emancipation and integration. This hierarchy places white women at the apex of beauty, rendering the aspiration to meet such standards not only unattainable for many, but also fundamentally unhealthy. Yet, it's puzzling to see how much of the Western world, and even Africa itself, aspires to a beauty standard that essentially appropriates these very traits that are inherent to Black women. As I delved into my research on beauty standards, I realized something striking. Many physical traits often deemed undesirable when associated with Blackness—such as full lips, large hips, and a curvaceous figure—are, in fact, widely coveted. However, when white people adopt these same features—full lips, curvy figures, tanned skin, and particular hairstyles—they become desirable trends. So, the notion of these features being "unappealing" reveals how beauty standards have been weaponized to diminish the attractiveness of Black women.

However, during the era when cotton was king, those who propagated the Southern economy—built on human livestock—found it advantageous to create a narrative that painted enslaved African women not only as undesirable, but also as brutish and hypersexual. This additional archetype was created to justify the breeding farms, which were common in the antebellum South after the end of the Transatlantic slave trade. The average enslaved woman at this time gave birth to her first child at age nineteen. And women and girls were forcefully impregnated for profit. Being able to commodify the Black woman's body has simultaneously created an archetype of both Jezebel as a sexual stereotype and the brute, or "Strong Black Woman," as a producer and worker. These false narratives that are enforced all around us in literature, film, and movies create a dichotomy so contradictory that the question itself becomes the ultimate gaslight—If Black is beautiful, why don't I see it reflected all around me? Why does it appear that Black women are not admired or valued in our true and authentic physical form?

Black feminist theory substantiates the claim that the devaluation of US Black women is rooted in the institution of American slavery. Black women's bodies were routinely violated for others' profit and pleasure without recourse or protection. During the era of American slavery, negative, controlling images of Black women emerged.[98] Black women were viewed as hypersexual Jezebels (or Sapphires) deserving of sexual exploitation, or as breeder women lawfully usable for populating owner's plantations with new slave stock or for revenue generation.

In the past and still today, Black women's bodies and beauty have largely been devalued and rejected by mainstream culture, which overvalues the European aesthetic and undervalues the aesthetic of other racial and ethnic groups, with the exception of exoticizing them.[99] The US puts a premium on "fair" white skin, blue eyes, and straight, long, blond hair. and considers these features the epitome of beauty. Features more akin to the African aesthetic are deemed ugly, undesirable, and less feminine. The notion that Black women are less attractive is a message that is transmitted daily by multiple external forces or social institutions (e.g., church, government, business industries, media, and family or peer groups).[100]

But it's important to understand that this is just that—a notion. It is a narrative that was created, much like racial hierarchy and colorism, to disempower and to plant the seed of self-hate and doubt that would advance European colonialism and imperialism. In the narrative of American beauty, Black women, adorned with historical scars, have often been overshadowed by Eurocentric ideals. Their intrinsic features, once marginalized, gained

---

98   hooks, bell. *Black looks: Race and Representations*. Toronto: Between the lines press, 1992.

99   Banks, 2000.

100 Awad, Germine H., Carolette Norwood, Desire S. Taylor, Mercedes Martinez, Shannon McClain, Bianca Jones, Andrea Holman, and Collette Chapman-Hilliard. 2015. "Beauty and Body Image Concerns Among African American College Women." *J Black Psychol* 41, no. 6 (December): 540–564.

limelight ironically when mirrored in lighter shades. Within Black communities too, the painful echoes of preference for lighter hues linger. African tresses, tales of pride and strength, face critique if they defy the straight line of Western approval.

Africa's philosophy of beauty is profound. Here, beauty isn't a mere surface reflection; it intertwines with worth, character, and societal roles. In this realm, beauty carries moral depth, reminiscent of the ancient Greek term *teleos*. Zimbabwe's *kunaka* and Nigeria's *ntuen-akpo* illustrate beauty as the union of character and charm. Beauty in Africa is communal, harmonizing societal norms, values, and ethos. The African belief, rooted in Ubuntu—"I am because we are"—views beauty as collective yet individualistic, thriving in community.

Historically, the essence of African womanhood has faced undeserved disdain, intensified post-colonization. The concept of "Blackness," created as a societal construct, further perpetuated this. In America, Black women have journeyed through the shadows of white-centric ideals since 1619. Their beauty, dissected by color and texture, was weighed against a foreign standard. Ironies abound: features shunned in Black women were celebrated in others. Historic tales painted Black women with conflicting images, both as overpowering and as overly sensual, often used to justify unspeakable horrors.

Literature and media have played into these narratives, further alienating Black women from their innate beauty. The mark of slavery, commodifying Black bodies, remains evident in contemporary culture. The question resonates: why isn't Black beauty universally celebrated?

Historical toys serve as a poignant illustration. As discussed above, prior to the 1950s, dolls reflective of African American grace were scarce. Such skewed portrayals impacted young Black psyches. The 1940s "doll tests" by the Clarks revealed the deep-seated impact of segregation on Black children's self-worth. Later, Margaret Beale Spencer's study, though with different tools, drew similar conclusions: societal biases still cast their haunting shadows on young minds.

#BlackGirlMagic arose as a beacon, empowering many. Yet, as the digital age evolves, society's beauty standards continue to challenge self-worth and acceptance. Understanding this dance with beauty is crucial, as it shapes self-perception, self-esteem, and the perpetual journey toward self-acceptance.

journaling questions

1. Reflecting on your childhood, how did the toys you played with and the media you consumed influence your perceptions of beauty, especially as it pertains to Black women?

2. Can you recall specific experiences where you encountered racial prejudice, and how did these incidents shape your self-perception and understanding of your place in the world?

3. How have prevailing societal views on Black beauty impacted your self-esteem throughout different stages of your life?

4. How has the #BlackGirlMagic movement influenced your perceptions of Black beauty and empowerment? Are there specific aspects of the movement that resonate with you deeply?

5. How familiar are you with the philosophical discourses on beauty within various African cultures? How might these perspectives provide alternative frameworks for understanding and embracing Black beauty?

6. In what ways have you observed the demonization or hypersexualization of African women in history and media? How do these portrayals contrast with your personal experiences and understandings of Black femininity?

7. How would you compare traditional African standards of beauty with contemporary global standards? How do you navigate and reconcile these potentially differing perspectives?

8. How have you seen the portrayal of Black women evolve in the media over the years? Are there changes that give you hope, or areas where you feel more progress is needed?

9. How do intersecting identities, such as sexuality, disability, or socioeconomic status, further complicate the narrative of Black beauty in society?

10. Considering the mixed messages from society and media about Black beauty, what messages or teachings would you want to pass on to younger Black women to ensure they grow up with a positive and empowered sense of self?

affirmations

1. I define my own standard of beauty, regardless of the limited representations in toys and media.

2. The prejudices I encounter do not define me. My worth is innate, and I stand tall in my truth.

3. Society's narrow view of beauty cannot diminish the vastness of my worth and the richness of my Black heritage.

4. I am a manifestation of #BlackGirlMagic, a testament to the strength, resilience, and beauty of Black women throughout history.

5. I draw strength from the deep-rooted African philosophies of beauty, recognizing that my essence is timeless and profound.

6. I reject any narrative that seeks to demonize or hypersexualize me. I honor the fullness of my identity, unapologetically.

7. My beauty, in its unique Black expression, is a celebration of history, culture, and individuality.

8. I am the storyteller of my own narrative, reclaiming my image from the distortions of history and media.

9. Together with my sisters, I build a community that uplifts, celebrates, and redefines standards of beauty on our own terms.

10. I am the legacy of generations of Black women who stood firm in their beauty and power. Their strength flows through me, and I honor it daily.

protecting my peace

identity, representation, & consequences of stereotypical portrayals

"I need to see my own beauty and to continue to be reminded that I am enough, that I am worthy of love without effort, that I am beautiful, that the texture of my hair and that the shape of my curves, the size of my lips, the color of my skin, and the feelings that I have are all worthy and okay."

—Tracee Ellis Ross

In the vast theater of societal perceptions, Black women often find themselves navigating the liminal spaces, those in-between realms where identity meets representation. The media, the powerful storyteller of our times, paints pictures that shape the collective psyche. For Black women, this canvas, historically marred by narrow perspectives, significantly impacts self-image.

Black women, with their multifaceted beauty and strength, have for centuries been framed within restrictive archetypes. From the indomitable "Mammy" to the hypersexualized "Jezebel," the media has often cast them into molds, sharply defined yet profoundly limiting. These depictions, more than mere celluloid images, infiltrate the mind, leaving traces on the soul.

The power of representation, especially in the media, is undeniable. It becomes the mirror wherein individuals see their reflections, gauge their worth, and discern their space in society. For Black women, historically, this mirror has been clouded, reflecting a distorted image shaped by Eurocentric ideals. Their full lips, curvaceous bodies, and coiled tresses, which once faced disdain or fetishization, suddenly became fashionable when sported by non-Black celebrities. Such disparities, subtle yet stinging, deeply affect one's self-perception.

Imagine the conundrum of a young Black girl navigating her self-worth in this labyrinth. The media showers accolades on features akin to hers, but only when they're presented on lighter, non-Black canvases. What does this tell her about her intrinsic value? That her beauty, in its authentic form, is lesser? This insidious message, though often unspoken, seeps into consciousness, shaping self-esteem.

Moreover, the media, with its far-reaching tendrils, often glorifies lighter skin, straight hair, and Eurocentric features as the epitome of beauty. In contrast, deeper hues and Afrocentric features find mention in passing or, worse, in negative contexts. Over time, these repeated images create an internalized belief system. The repercussions? A surge in skin-lightening products, hair relaxers, and a haunting quest to fit into a mold not one's own.

Yet, the poetic irony lies herein: Black culture, in all its vibrancy, has been the bedrock of global trends. Music, dance, fashion—its influence is pervasive. However, the very progenitors of this rich tapestry, Black women themselves, often find their contributions sidelined or appropriated, their essence diluted.

But it's not all shadows. As dawn breaks, there's a stirring renaissance. Today's media landscape is gradually shifting, led by fierce Black women who reclaim their narratives. From luminous screen queens like Viola Davis and Lupita Nyong'o to influential authors like Chimamanda Ngozi Adichie, Black women are carving out spaces where their stories resonate in their authentic voice. The #BlackGirlMagic movement, an ode to Black femininity and strength, further punctuates this era of self-affirmation.

Yet, one must not mistake this reclamation as mere trend. It's a powerful, resonant call to rectify centuries of misrepresentation. It's a reminder that Black beauty is not monolithic, not a stereotype to be compartmentalized, but a spectrum, diverse and radiant.

Therefore, the interplay of societal perceptions and media representation has wielded a profound impact on the self-image of Black women. Historically skewed toward limiting archetypes and Eurocentric ideals, it has shaped self-perception, often to detrimental effects. Yet, the contemporary narrative is evolving, marked by empowerment and self-affirmation. In this tapestry of change, the onus is on society at large to champion this shift, ensuring that every Black woman sees her reflection, not as society dictates, but in her unadulterated, resplendent truth.

Award-winning actress Viola Davis expresses concern about this messaging in mainstream media and culture after becoming the first African American to win an Emmy for best actress in a drama. Her acceptance speech places her award within the larger context of diversity in Hollywood:

> In my mind, I see a line. And over that line, I see green fields and lovely flowers and beautiful white women with their arms stretched out to me, over that line. But I can't seem to get there no how. I can't seem to get over that line.
>
> That was Harriet Tubman in the 1800s. And let me tell you something: The only thing that separates women of color from anyone else is opportunity.
>
> You cannot win an Emmy for roles that are simply not there. So here's to all the writers, the awesome people that are Ben Sherwood, Paul Lee, Peter Nowalk, Shonda Rhimes, people who have redefined what it means to be beautiful, to be sexy, to be a leading woman, to be Black.
>
> And to the Taraji P. Hensons, the Kerry Washingtons, the Halle Berrys, the Nicole Beharies, the Meagan Goods, to Gabrielle Union: Thank you for taking us over that line.[101]

The Geena Davis Institute on Gender in Media's tagline, "If you can see it, you can be it," aptly encapsulates the struggle for representation and appreciation of Black women in the media. The nonprofit organization recently conducted a study titled 'Representations of Black Women in Hollywood,' which examines the representation of Black women and girls in entertainment media. Much of the existing research on race and gender in entertainment media analyzes representations of women and Black people as two distinct groups, but far less is known about the intersectional depictions of Black girls and women in Hollywood. It is important to note that the number of Black female characters

---

101 Gold, Michael. 2023. "Viola Davis's Emmy Speech." *New York Times,* March 4, 2023. archive.nytimes. com/www.nytimes.com/live/emmys-2015/viola-daviss-emotional-emmys-acceptance-speech/.

in film and on TV is too small to examine Black women and girls separately, so the analysis was combined.

In analyzing the study reports, it's clear to see that, no matter the arguments to the contrary, representation of Black women, Black beauty, and authentic portrayals of Blackness, including natural hair, are severely lacking throughout the media. There is a void in telling our stories in any meaningful way. Physical representation should be a natural extension of any attention or value placed on these stories. It is noticeably absent, and this begins to permeate our self-concept. Ultimately, our self-esteem and self-confidence suffer. This gradual erosion, which begins when we are very young, is barely noticeable. The lack of dolls that resemble us, societal pressure to straighten our natural hair in order to fit in, and the pervasive whitewashed perception of beauty all subtly reinforce it. We are made aware at a very young age that we *are not* that.

According to the study, Black girls and women make up 6.5 percent of the US population, but only 3.7 percent of leads and co-leads in the hundred top-grossing films of the last decade. Sadly, this figure represents an improvement from previous years, when it was even lower. Only one in five (19.0 percent) of Black leading ladies from the past decade have a dark skin tone. Furthermore, most Black leading ladies (57.1 percent) from popular films in the past decade are depicted with hairstyles that conform to European standards of beauty as opposed to natural Black hairstyles.

When it comes to sexualization, Black women (13.5 percent) and other women of color (14.8 percent) are depicted as partially or fully nude more often than their white counterparts (9.0 percent). Moreover, other women of color (56.9 percent) and white women (51.2 percent) are significantly more likely to be depicted as attractive than Black women (41.4 percent) in family films. Finally, Black female characters are more likely to be depicted as violent than white female characters (29.3 percent compared to 24.6 percent) and twice as likely to be portrayed as violent as other female characters of color (14.8 percent).

A similar pattern regarding the representation of Black women on family television is revealed in the study. Black female characters and other female characters of color are twice as likely as white female characters to be shown with a degree of nudity (5.2 percent and 4.9 percent, compared with 2.5 percent). Compared to white female characters, Black female characters and other female characters of color are twice as likely to be shown in revealing clothing (10.7 percent and 8.7 percent, compared with 4.5 percent). In addition, Black female characters are more likely than white female characters and other female characters of color to be verbally objectified by other characters in family TV (1.4 percent compared with 0.5 percent and 0.6 percent, respectively).

The study also found that White female characters are more likely to have an occupation (89.6 percent) than Black female characters (70.5 percent) or other female characters of color (58.8 percent). Additionally, Black female characters are twice as likely as white female characters and other female characters of color to be depicted in a service industry job (56.3 percent, compared to 26.4 percent and 20.6 percent, respectively). Finally, Black women (5.6 percent) are less likely than white women (8.7 percent) and other women of color (11.0 percent) to be shown in a romantic relationship, but more likely to be shown as having at least one sexual partner. Black women are more than twice as likely to have at least one sexual partner in family films as in family TV (13.3 percent compared with 5.1 percent).[102]

A 2022 report, conducted by the NAACP Hollywood Bureau, Dr. Darnell Hunt, Dean of Social Sciences at UCLA, and Motivational Educational Entertainment (MEE) Production, emphasizes that the lack of Black executives on media teams can be harmful to audiences. The report also points out that there weren't any Black chief executive officers (CEOs) or members of the senior management

---

102   Geena Davis Institute on Gender in Media. 2023. "Representations of Black Women in Hollywood—Geena Davis Institute." Geena Davis Institute on Gender in Media. seejane.org/research-informs-empowers/representations-of-black-women-in-hollywood/.

team at the major studios in 2020, and only 3.9 percent of major studio unit heads were Black.

Continued and positive representation—both behind the scenes and on screen—can have an effect on the Black community, particularly its youth. Representation in the media is important for several reasons, ranging from positive changes in physical health to a decline in racial profiling.

Research from the Urban Institute's 2017 Trusted Source explains how the media can influence health behaviors. If that's true, then the lack of representation—both overall and positive—can impact the overall health of Black people. Certain demographics—such as white, heterosexual, cisgender, male, and Christian—are considered the dominant culture. So, people who fall outside those groups can often be left behind when it comes to representation.

The NAACP study states, "The most damaging consequence of the industry's faulty approximation of genuine Black experiences is the absorption and adoption of those characterizations as misshapen forms of self-identity, worthy of emulation."

Discussing the lack of accuracy in media portrayals, Deidre White, a licensed marriage and family therapist in Georgia, states, "The negative effects on Black individuals are direct, stemming from the consumption of harmful messages that shape attitudes and behaviors. The impact of these harmful messages could be lessened with increased representation both on screen and behind the scenes."

Alton Bozeman, a psychologist with the Menninger Clinic, points out that stereotypical representations, which are ingrained and widespread, tend to overlook the importance of authentic and diverse representation. Black characters in movies and TV often end up as side characters or vehicles to further white character arcs. "It's not enough for characters, news anchors, or nonfictional subjects to be present and visible," he says. "It's also important that these portrayals are relatable." Bozeman adds, "What makes them relatable is the authenticity of character to one's culture in the case of fictional characters. In the case of news personalities and nonfictional personalities, it's the positivity of the portrayals that matters most."

Keischa Pruden, LCMHC and founder of Pruden Counseling Concepts, discusses how Black people have endured stereotypes for hundreds of years, including their portrayal via harmful stereotypes such as being violent, lazy, or negligent parents. Pruden says, "...young people are the most influenced by what they see, read, and listen to [and] find examples of how to walk, talk, music to listen to, ideas to live by... It would seem imperative that our young Black people be afforded the opportunity to see representations of themselves in a positive, affirming light."

Angela Robinson, LPC, a clinical director of NorthNode Counseling, says, "We're constantly told negative things within our family systems, society, and throughout history that can oftentimes keep us caged in, in regards to thinking."

A 2003 article discussed this negative and stereotypical media representation of Black people and spoke about the prevalence of the portrayals of Black men in TV and movies as dangerous criminals and the potential connection to societal perception mirroring these stereotypes.

The NAACP report confirmed these observations. The report specifically states that media content, whether accurate or not, shapes opinions about Black people, which ultimately influences perceptions, behaviors, and even laws and policies. These, in turn, have significant psychological and emotional impacts on social circumstances. Pruden spoke about the messages that can be conveyed to young Black kids when they don't see themselves represented, whether or not the message is overt. " 'You're not important to share with the world.' 'You're not skilled enough to be in front or behind the camera.' 'Your story doesn't have relevance.' Imagine being a young child and receiving those types of messages,"

Pruden says. "Whether implied or stated outright, negative messages keep children from chasing dreams, seeing their potential, and feeling good about themselves."[103]

So this is why we say beauty is more than skin deep. It's probably why, when the podcast host asked, I couldn't recall a time when I felt truly beautiful. Even the word "beauty" doesn't fully connect with me in describing how I feel my image is perceived in the world and my perception of myself. There is a part of me that has always felt otherworldly. In some ways, that has been a way to boost my self-esteem—by proclaiming that Black girls are, indeed, magical. But for many of us, in the years since George Floyd's murder, the racial reckoning that wasn't quite giving, and the following years of broken promises, we don't have the sustained energy required for "magic." We simply wish to exist, asking, "Why can't we just live?" We desire acceptance as regular individuals, not as extraordinary or "magical." We desire to feel whole and not marginalized simply for being who we are. Yet, we find that our physical characteristics or ethnicity often become a symbolic statement that overshadows our individual identities.

In addition, the pervasive hypersexualization of Black women in the media significantly influences the philosophies imparted to us by our parents, grandparents, and other community members during our childhood. Black girls are told to focus on books and not their beauty. We are expected to concentrate on building the skills to pay the bills—beauty is not considered one of them! This frames our behavior and how we navigate the world around us. We shrink from attention, brush off compliments, mute our bold lipstick, or try to tame our glorious crowns of 4C coils.

Consequently, considering ourselves beautiful, pampering ourselves, and loving the skin we are in seems frivolous. Many of us abandon those practices once

103 Johnson, Jacquelyn, Taneasha White, and Bailey Mariner. 2022. "NAACP Report: Impact of the Lack of Black Hollywood Execs." Psych Central. psychcentral.com/health/the-absence-of-black-executives-in-hollywood-naacp-report.

we become grown women and struggle to find the time, space, and energy to celebrate our own beauty. Even when we do, there is still a nagging sense that it doesn't measure up to society's standard, although intellectually we know that is not the truth. Sometimes we feel that we should adapt to those same standards, although we're not exactly sure why.

Our eyes tell us something is amiss based on the world around us, and our emotions respond in kind. For us, the effect it has on our psyches is devastating, although we may not be aware of it. We often feel as though our identity is invisible to others unless we actively assert it. This sense of isolation and not belonging in the world follows us persistently, like a shadow. Although we tell ourselves we are beautiful, there's a nagging feeling of sadness when an actress plays a role in a movie or television show, illustrating what you've been looking for all your life, only to see her not accepted or acknowledged for her work.

It all goes back to the heart of the beauty of the Black woman, which transcends the physical, and how it's vitally necessary as a source of strength for the entire community. Studies show that the lack of media representation and not seeing our Black beauty reflected around us are particularly harmful for Black women. But few studies have been done to explore specifically how Black women are affected by this phenomenon.

Historically, Black women's oppression has taken three forms: economic, political, and through negative controlling images. How Black women respond to that oppression is best understood through the lens of Black feminist theory. As an academic specializing in race, class, and gender, Patricia Hill Collins is a distinguished university professor of sociology emerita at the University of Maryland, College Park. She and others have noted that one such response is to internalize these racist messages that decree Black women second-rate and abnormal based on the White standard. Internalized racism is a prominent theme in Black literature (e.g., novelists such as George Schulyer, James Baldwin, Zora Neale Hurston, Gwendolyn Brooks, and Toni Morrison).[104]

A recent study conducted at a large southwestern university confirms that young Black women often feel constrained and devalued by white beauty standards, which celebrate features and aesthetics that are typically unattainable for them. Despite prior studies that suggest Black women have high esteem when it comes to body image attitudes, these data amply demonstrate that Black women struggle daily with reconciling their beauty with that of mainstream standards. Black women feel like they are constantly assaulted (blatant and latent) for their perceived "ugliness" by the media, peers, and even family.[105]

In keeping with Black feminist theory, one of the ways some of these women cope with these microaggressions and invalidations is to redefine or self-define a beauty standard that is not at odds with their own aesthetic.[106] To illustrate this point, one respondent notes:

> As long as I perceive myself as beautiful, then I really don't have any issues with the media's definition of beautiful or how others would define beauty or just anything that goes along with that type of reference just because of what's in the media today and what image, like what the younger generation's going through. And even just us, what you always see in the magazine or the TV. If you don't have that self-image, then you might not be satisfied with yourself.[107]

104 Collins, Patricia H. 1990. *Black Feminist Thought: Knowledge, Consciousness and the Politics of Empowerment.* London: HarperCollins.

105 Awad GH, Norwood C, Taylor DS, Martinez M, McClain S, Jones B, Holman A, Chapman-Hilliard C. Beauty and Body Image Concerns Among African American College Women. J Black Psychol. 2015 Dec 1;41(6):540-564. doi: 10.1177/0095798414550864. Epub 2014 Nov 12. PMID: 26778866; PMCID: PMC4713035.

106 Collins, 1990.

107 Awad et al., 2015.

According to Dr. Christine C. Iijima Hall, an expert in this area, feelings of inadequacy and inferiority about personal beauty emerge as major themes in the mental health treatment of African American women.[108] These themes are both historical and sociopolitical. She explains that Black women may be additionally vulnerable due to the double jeopardy of racism and sexism in the American beauty standard.[109] This, compounded with discrimination, can cause "insidious trauma"[110] and if prolonged, may lead to reactions resembling post-traumatic stress disorder.[111] In fact, psychologists of color have even begun to view racism as a form of long-term terrorism.[112]

Dr. Hall suggests that members of the Black community consider several strategies, including teaching children to critically evaluate the white beauty standards often propagated in the media and society. Since "beauty is...a result of societal indoctrination," according to sociocultural theory,[113] beauty can be indoctrinated in a positive direction by a nurturing environment. For example, Gitter and O'Connell[114] found that doll color preference could be changed by differentially rewarding children who chose the dark doll. The Black community, and particularly the Black family, may need to strongly reinforce the positive African image. Dr. Hall also recommends community activities that increase ethnic pride.

Other options appropriate for addressing the issue of body image with African American women include a better understanding of the political and social realities

108 Boyd-Franklin, Nancy. 1991. "Recurrent themes in the treatment of African American women in group psychotherapy." *Women & Therapy* 11 (2): 25–40. DOI: 10.1300/J015V11N02_04.

109 hooks, 1992.

110 Root, Maria P. 1990. "Disordered eating in women of color." *Sex Roles* 22:525–536.

111 Comas-Diaz, L. 1994. "LatiNegra: Mental health issues of African Latinas." *Journal of Feminist Family Therapy* 5:35–64.

112 Wyatt, G. 1989. *The terrorism of racism: Effects on ethnic minorities,* Invited address at the American Psychological Association Annual Convention.

113 Bond, Selena, and Thomas F. Cash. 1992. "Black beauty: Skin color and body image among African American college women." *Journal of Applied Social Psychology,* 874–888.

114 Gitter, George, and Stephen M. McConnell. 1970. "Racial appearance of ideal blacks." *CRC Report* 48:1–20.

while obtaining tools with which to fight an oppressive society. Culturally relevant therapy that addresses the issues of oppression, powerlessness, and racist and sexist "insidious trauma" can provide a Black woman with awareness of the external forces affecting her body image and coping mechanisms.[115]

This can also be accomplished through individual and/or group therapy. Nancy Boyd-Franklin[116] has found support groups with Black women who share similar experiences to be extremely successful. She reports that these groups tend to help each other "gain important insight into these unconscious triggers, fears, anger and resentment..." Women can express these feelings toward society, and perhaps toward the family, that create negative perceptions of their bodies, skin, hair, and facial features. Once this process is completed, African American women may be better prepared to deal with discrimination in the future.[117]

Political and economic involvement is yet another therapeutic intervention for women of color. Activism not only empowers people so they are less likely to feel helpless; it can also lead to societal changes. Ethnic women's responses to white beauty standards cannot be viewed as an esoteric or pathologically narcissistic issue. Issues of racism, sexism, poverty, and other forms of discrimination affect women of color in various ways. Negative body image is simply one by-product of a society that does not recognize the social, scientific, professional, and political contributions of African American women.[118]

When we think about ways to empower ourselves and assert our own value, we must remember our beautiful cultural tradition of using beauty as a resource to uplift the community. It's also crucial to acknowledge that research, historical

~~~~~~~~

115 Root, 1990.

116 Boyd-Franklin, 1991. 4.

117 Jackson, Leslie C., and Beverly Greene. 2000. *Psychotherapy with African American women: innovations in psychodynamic perspectives and practice.* New York: Guilford Press.

118 Ijima Hall, Christine C. 1995. "Beauty is in the soul of the beholder: Psychological implications of beauty and African American women." *Cultural Diversity and Mental Health* 1 (2): 125–137.

backgrounds, and studies show Black women are overwhelmingly negatively affected by various factors. These include the lack of representation and erasure of our beauty in mainstream media, the lack of cosmetic options that cater to our needs, and the negative stereotypes that plague our identities. With growing awareness of my history, my activism and confidence blossomed, leading me to perceive my beauty in a way that transcends mere physical appearance. I began to feel beautiful because I knew I was uplifting other Black women in everything I did. The glow up was for each and every Black woman I interacted with.

And my own journey is still one of growth and discovery in exploring how I react to the world and how to work on the process of decolonizing my own mind. Understanding the historical reasons behind the use of meaningless archetypes to frame Black womanhood helped put my feelings of discontent into context. I was not alone in how I felt. This has been going on since the beginning of our existence in the Western hemisphere. Women across the African diaspora have been viewed as commodities, and our beauty has been fetishized, marginalized, and appropriated without our permission or acknowledgment of just how central our beauty is to popular culture.

For many of us, the relentless campaign to erase Black beauty leaves us feeling marginalized and invisible. Struggling to find makeup that matches our skin tones is more than an inconvenience; it's a blatant manifestation of racial bias. Similarly, the lack of representation in beauty standards is deeply disconcerting and alienating. But we have started to see Black female entrepreneurs embark on a mission to bring Black beauty into the mainstream retail market. Seeing our images, products designed for us, and marketing that speaks to our unique needs, we are able to feel validated and, most of all, to feel as beautiful on the outside as we know we are both inside and out.

I have had the opportunity to engage with individuals who are combating these issues head-on. For example, during an episode of the Black Power Moves podcast, I had the opportunity to interview KJ Miller, cofounder of Mented

Cosmetics. This multimillion-dollar cosmetics company that Miller and her partner founded focuses on offering a selection of lipsticks and other beauty products especially made for women of color in an effort to provide access to cosmetics that work with different skin tones. She created the first lipstick by whipping up the formula in her kitchen and launched it in 2017 with fellow Harvard graduate Amanda E. Johnson. Their mission, as stated on their website, is inclusive and empowering: "Mented exists to celebrate all hues and to make beauty truly, wonderfully inclusive. We created Mented Cosmetics because we believe everyone should be able to find themselves in the world of beauty, no matter your skin tone. We know you'll love being put first—because when it comes to beauty, no one deserves to be an afterthought."

The makeup brand started as a conversation with her friend and cofounder about the products they wanted as Black women, but didn't see available in the market.

> I was working as a consultant. I was traveling every week. I was on the road Monday to Thursday. So we would get together on the weekends and just talk about, what are our problems? [...] What don't we have that we wish we had?

> What could we be good at together? And during one of those conversations, she mentioned she'd been looking for the perfect nude lipstick for three years. [...] And I was like, "Girl, I can't find any lipstick that works for me, much less a nude lipstick." And so that, for both of us, was kind of the moment where we said, [...] there's something here, because here we are, two women with disposable income who want to be spending our money on beauty, but who keep running up against this wall. We keep feeling disappointed by the beauty experience.

> We can't find a brand that seems to be speaking to us, and we certainly can't find a brand that seems to be prioritizing us. And don't we all deserve to be prioritized by the brands we're spending money on? And so then we started

surveying our friends and our family and asking them, well, look, [...] are you happy with the beauty brands you're spending money on? Do you feel prioritized? Do you feel celebrated?

And over and over again, we kept hearing no. And so that really led us to believe there was a real opportunity here. And so we said, okay, well, let's start with nude lipstick, because that seems to be a real problem area. [...] And look, neither of us had ever made nude lipstick, but [...] we figured, how hard could it be? [...] It's not rocket science.

And so we started by thinking we should go to a manufacturer. But when we started reaching out to manufacturers, they didn't really get it. They were like nude lipsticks. Yeah, we got those. We got plenty of nude lipsticks. And so they would send us their stock shades. And we were like, no, these are the nude lipsticks that don't work. These are the ashy nude lipsticks. These are the pale nude lips. [...] These are the ones we don't want.

And they were like, well, we can tweak them. And we were like, but if we start with something that doesn't work, [...] how are we going to make it work? Do you see how that doesn't make sense? [...] We don't want to start with something bad and try to make it good. And so [...] we said, we have to do it ourselves.

And so we literally went to YouTube and found videos of girls making lipsticks on their own and said, we can do that. And so then we ordered the products. We ordered the oils, the waxes, the micas, the colorants, [...] the molds, and we made them. And on our first try, on our first night, we came up with our two top selling shades that are still our two top selling shades today. We've made millions of dollars on those shades, and we made them on our first night.

So it wasn't that it couldn't be done. It's that people didn't want to, brands didn't want to. [...] And [...] all these years later, [...] I say all these years, five years later, [...] I still think back to that, because [...] to me, what it shows is [...] this industry and this industry now has moved much more in the right direction. But when we were getting started, they were really skating by on [...] essentially [...] doing the bare minimum. And now they can't get away with that because too many customers, too many people have said the bare minimum isn't good enough.

And I like to think that Mented is part of the reason a lot of these brands aren't getting away with doing the bare minimum anymore. [...] But that's how we got started. We said, look, if they're not going to do it, let's do it. [...] The way I got started was just being the sort of person who's willing to fail until I succeed.

We had our prototypes and we marched them into a lot of rooms and said, look, what you're seeing before you is a handmade prototype. But what it's going to be is a multimillion-dollar business that women around the world are going to fall in love with. But right now, it's a handmade prototype. [...] So [...] we had to sell them on the vision; we had to sell them on the story.

And that means that we had to be our biggest cheerleaders. We couldn't walk in and say, [...] here's this lipstick. It's great. We had to say [...] Black women have been neglected for decades, but we outspend our white counterparts on beauty by upwards of 80 percent. So imagine what this brand is going to be worth. Imagine how much she's going to be willing to spend when I put a lipstick that was made for her in front of her, right?

That's what we had to say. And that's how you convince people that it's worth it to work with you. When you're placing a two-thousand-unit order, when a homeboy down the street is placing a half-a-million-unit order, right? So it takes a lot of grit, and luckily we have that.[119]

Therefore, for Black women, often the crafting of our own beauty image and understanding that, although we navigate a society that doesn't tend to reflect our physical beauty, our beauty radiates from within, is crucial. In KJ Miller's case, it came from a passion for entrepreneurship, a love of Black women and our needs, and finding ways to meet those needs. For many of us, it comes from the images we see on social media that tend to be more representative of our cultural aesthetic. as well as from the images we surround ourselves with on a daily basis. The walls of my home office are filled with images of and affirmations about Black beauty and African culture. I want every moment I can to reinforce, in both my intentional consumption of images reflecting my beauty as well as affirming and validating it to myself, that I am perfectly and wonderfully made. Being intentional in that practice has been one of the foundational ways of increasing my emotional well-being and boosting my confidence in my day-to-day interactions with people in the majority who do not look like me.

To celebrate my own beauty and Blackness, I intentionally immersed myself in the African diaspora's concept of beauty. This emphasis on traditional beauty celebrated within our Black community has not only enriched my personal understanding but also underscored the broader societal discourse. I am every Black woman who came before me, and I am every Black woman who will come after me. Centering our culture and focusing on the beauty that resides within it keeps me glowing, with melanin popping every single day.

Being intentional about this practice is essential to countering the negative images and stereotypes we encounter. A particular moment on *The Unlearning with Lindsey T. H. Jackson* series sparked introspection for me. The host asked

---

119 Miller, KJ. 2022. "Making of a Pigment-First Beauty Brand Celebrating All Hues." Edited by Elizabeth Leiba. In *Black Power Moves*. Spotify. Interview. open.spotify.com/episode/7v9itq0Q3s N4V392VQUxHE?si=Eom95ZczRsyO5P5-nKGgVQ.

a question I found myself unable to answer: "When was the last time you felt beautiful?" In the weeks that followed, I grappled with that silence. I decided to stop waiting for others' validation, a scarcity in the predominantly white spaces we navigate today. Instead, I started by telling myself I was beautiful in the mirror every morning. Initially, very simply, "You know what? You're pretty!" I flashed a brilliant white smile at my reflection. I winked at myself. I poked out my tongue and crossed my eyes! I blew myself kisses. I wanted to counteract anything and everything I would see in the world that day that told me otherwise. I wanted to remind myself how much there is to love about the face I see looking back at me in the mirror.

Tracey Owens Patton, Director of African American and Diaspora Studies and a professor of communication in the Department of Communication and Journalism at the University of Wyoming, is a notable figure in this discussion. She advocates for using Afrocentric theory as a tool to challenge the hegemonic White standard of beauty through Black beauty liberation. Afrocentric theory is used in a dynamic way that allows one to look at the beauty diversity within Black women, instead of treating all Black women as a monolithic group. As with standpoint theory, which encourages viewing the world from the perspectives of marginalized groups, Afrocentric theory empowers individuals to assert their own experiences and identities, thereby resisting the dominance of mainstream culture. Finally, Afrocentric theory allows one to see the diversity among Black women in terms of body image, body size, hair, and skin color because of the focus on valuing the personal experience, allowing one to name and define her own experience(s). Through embracing alternatives, Afrocentric theory shatters the myth that Black women constitute a monolithic group because one is allowed to consider intragroup diversity.

With its focus on humanity, the diversity one can find through Afrocentric theory is transformative. Afrocentric theory is important because it "embraces an alternative set of realities, experiences, and identities."[120] One need not necessarily be African or African American to embrace Afrocentricity and conduct Afrocentric research.[121] Not only can a woman exercise agency with her beauty choices, but Afrocentricity creates a performative space of creativity and acceptance that has room for all types of beauty because it is no longer in the context of a Euro-supremacist framework. There is not an adherence to any beauty standard, but a celebration of the self. This celebration of self is challenged by Eurocentric beauty standards of body image, hair, and race.[122]

Make no mistake about it, one of the beautiful things about Afrocentric theory is the recognition that Black folk are not a monolith, and by extension, Black women and our perceptions of ourselves reside in the framework of beauty outside the construct of a white Eurocentric lens. For Black women, this means that we can be united in the understanding that, despite different shades of melanin, hair textures, and choices in how we style our hair, or even our body shape and size, we can choose to express our beauty in any way that feels right to us in our creative celebration of a beauty that radiates from within. By embracing this philosophy, we are no longer the proverbial Jiggaboos versus Wannabes, like the feuding factions of college students in Spike Lee's *School Daze*. We reject the destructive construct of colorism, which has been used as a weapon to favor lighter skin tones. This preference is based on a flawed idea that proximity to whiteness is somehow better, but we know that's a fallacy. Our beauty doesn't need validation from such arbitrary standards. We can never be them, and wouldn't want to be even if we could. But we have to stop molding our beauty standards around what is unattainable, even if only in some subconscious desire to be seen and validated. No more good hair. No more light eyes make you a prize.

120 Delgado, Fernando P. 1998. "When the Silenced Speak: The Textualization and Complications of Latino/a Identity." *Western Journal of Communication* 62(4):420–38. 62 (4): 420–438.

121 Asante, Molefi K. 1991. "The Afrocentric Idea in Education." *Journal of Negro Education* 60 (2): 170–180.

122 Owens Patton, Tracey. 2006. "Hey Girl, Am I More than My Hair?: African American Women and Their Struggles with Beauty, Body Image, and Hair." *NWSA Journal* 18, no. 2 (Summer): 26–27.

But conversely, no more weave-shaming or fat-shaming. Instead, we should embrace the beauty we already have in such abundance that our sun-kissed skin has been admired for ages, since the very beginning of time.

I've been known to rock a good wig—burgundy, pink, or honey brown. I used to buy Brazilian hair at a huge store in South Miami, where they sewed the hair right on the weft. I've had *Poetic Justice* jumbo braids, beautiful Bantu knots, and microbraids that took seven hours. I refused to take them out forever because I needed to get my money's worth and couldn't find anyone to help me!

I've worn twist-outs, braid-outs, afros, roller sets, blow-outs, cornrows, and knotless plaits. I don't think there is a type of hair style or a way of wearing my hair, natural or otherwise, that I haven't tried. But I've definitely always had a rather tenuous relationship with my hair. Always praying for it to grow, then cutting it off because I couldn't figure out what to do with it. Or it was getting on my nerves. Or it was too expensive to go to the salon every week, wasting my precious time and money for a wash and set to maintain my laid-and-slayed top-shelf relaxer.

I did my first big chop in 2005. It was the beginning of the natural-hair movement, and social media had just begun to take off. I watched YouTube relentlessly, finding natural-hair gurus who would bring me to the promised land of embracing the true texture of my hair. I was anxious to learn more about the hair that sprouted from my scalp. I had never seen it or touched it as an adult. I couldn't remember the texture except from vague memories of sitting between my mother's legs on the floor as she meticulously braided it. And of course, the times when she permitted me to have it straightened for a special occasion. But thinking about how special it felt when she would slowly comb through my curls and intricately braid my tresses was intriguing to me. I wanted to recapture that feeling for myself.

Finally, we come to our crowning glory in our exploration of self-image, shaped by beauty standards imposed by a society where we have been both racialized and minoritized. At the top of our heads is our halo of hair, which defies gravity! Most of us, as Black women, have had a conflicted relationship with our curls since childhood. We have often seen our hair as part of the friction we have to navigate in an already complicated world. Our hair is part creative expression, but it has to be tamed to meet the expectations of society. It is part of our Black pride and can also create discomfort, shame, or anxiety about its perception by those in the majority. It grows out of our heads and is a part of us, but it is also seen as a radical form of political expression. And the hair of Black women across the African diaspora has historically had great traditional and cultural significance.

As far back as the early fifteenth century, hairstyles carried rich symbolism within our communities. For tribes like the Wolof, Mende, Mandingo, and Yoruba, the way one wore their hair could tell a story of age, ethnic identity, marital status, community rank, religious beliefs, status in war, and wealth. Hair styling sessions were a bonding time for women. A hairstylist, with their intricate knowledge of the cultural significance and techniques of hair grooming, always held a prominent position in these communities. "The complicated and time-consuming task of hair grooming included washing, combing, oiling, braiding, twisting, and/or decorating the hair with any number of adornments, including cloth, beads, and shells. The process could last several hours, sometimes several days."

As the world began to globalize and cultures intersected, the significance of these hairstyles came into play. The most common hairstyles Europeans encountered when they began exploring the western coast of Africa in the mid-1400s included "braids, plaits, patterns shaved into the scalp, and any combination of shells, flowers, beads, or strips of material woven into the hair." During this time period, hair was not only a cosmetic concern, but "its social, aesthetic, and spiritual significance has been intrinsic to their sense of self for thousands of years." However, with the tragic advent of the Atlantic slave trade, the cultural significance of hair became a target. Realizing the prominent role hair played in the lives of western Africans, the first thing enslavers did was shave their heads. This was an unspeakable crime for Africans because the people were shorn of their identity.

Throughout the centuries of slavery, scarves became a practical alternative for covering kinky, unstyled hair or hair that suffered from patchy baldness, breakage, or disease. In households, various materials like bacon grease and butter were used to condition and soften the hair, prepare it for straightening, and make it shine. Cornmeal and kerosene were used as scalp cleaners, and coffee became a natural dye for women.

The type of work that enslaved Africans did frequently determined their hairstyles. If they were in the field and lived in separate slave quarters, "the women wore head rags, and the men took to shaving their heads, wearing straw hats, or using animal shears to cut their hair short." If enslaved Africans worked directly with the white population in roles such as barbers, cooks, or housekeepers, they often styled their hair similarly to their white counterparts. For example, if they worked in the "big house," they were required to have a "neat and tidy appearance or risk the wrath of the master, so men and women wore tight braids, plaits, and cornrows."

The forced adoption of white hairstyles, especially straight hair, held a multitude of implications within the Black community. It wasn't so much a preference as a survival strategy; straighter hair was often associated with the status of a free person. Light-skinned enslaved Africans who managed to escape "tried to pass themselves off as free, hoping their European features would be enough to convince bounty hunters that they belonged to that privileged class." According to historians, emulating whiteness offered a certain amount of protection. In addition, enslaved individuals who were lighter-skinned and had straighter hair often worked inside the plantation houses. This work was generally less physically demanding than the tasks assigned to slaves in the fields. These individuals also had better access to clothes, education, and food. Sometimes, they were even promised freedom upon the master's death.

However, the "jealous mistress of the manor often shaved off the [light-skinned female house slave's] lustrous mane of hair [as a punishment], indicating that white women too understood the significance of long, kink-free hair." So, adopting many white European traits was essential to survival, e.g., free vs. slave; employed vs. unemployed; educated vs. uneducated; upper class vs. poor.

Opinions about hair straightening were split within the Black community. Some viewed it as an unfortunate attempt to emulate white standards, equating the practice with self-hatred and shame.[123] However, most Black women felt straightened hairstyles were not about emulating whites, but having modern hairstyles. Madame C. J. Walker was one of the more popularly known hair stylists who helped African American women achieve modern hairstyles. In the twentieth century, the 1905 invention of Madame C. J. Walker's hair softener, which accompanied a hair-straightening comb, was all the rage. Hair straightening was a way to challenge the predominant nineteenth-century belief that Black beauty was ugly. According to Noliwe Rooks, academic, author, and the L. Herbert Ballou University Professor and chair of Africana Studies at Brown University, "Due to pressure from society, African Americans struggled with issues of inferiority, beauty, and the meaning of particular beauty practices. Walker attempted to shift the significance of hair away from concerns about disavowing African ancestry."[124]

Hair straightening has continued to be a controversial beauty move by some in the African American community, particularly after the 1960s and 1970s "Black is Beautiful" social movement. For example, Malcolm X spoke out against hair

123 Byrd, Ayana D., and Lori L. Tharps. 2001. *Hair Story: Untangling the Roots of Black Hair in America.* New York: St. Martin's Griffin.

124 Rooks, Noliwe. 1996. *Hair Raising.* New Jersey: Rutgers University Press.

straightening. He believed that it caused Black people to feel ashamed of their natural beauty and was a means to emulate white standards of beauty.[125]

The "conk" was a major plot device in Spike Lee's film biography of Malcolm X, based upon Malcolm X's own condemnation of the hairstyle in his autobiography, due to its implications of the superiority of a more "white" appearance and because of the pain the process causes and the possibility of receiving severe burns to the scalp.[126] We probably all remember the famous scene from the movie *Malcolm X*, where actor Denzel Washington plays the title role and demonstrates the torturous process of straightening his hair into a "conk." The conk was a hairstyle popular among African American men from the 1920s up to the early to mid-1960s. Conks were often styled as large pompadours, although other men chose to simply slick their straightened hair back, allowing it to lie flat on their heads. Regardless of the styling, conks required a considerable amount of effort to maintain; a man often had to wear a do-rag of some sort at home to absorb sweat or other agents to keep them from causing his hair to revert prematurely to its natural state.[127]

The conk involved chemically straightening naturally "kinky" hair with a homemade gel relaxer known as congolene. The process was complex and required considerable care and maintenance. The initially homemade hair straightener gel was made from the extremely corrosive chemical lye, which was often mixed with eggs and potatoes. The hairstylist had to wear gloves, and the solution exposure was timed just right on the client's head and then thoroughly rinsed out with cold water to avoid chemical burns. Malcolm X's reflections serve as a stark reminder of how much these standards have influenced our sense of identity—often to the point where we feel lost—by pressuring us to conform and alter our natural features. It underlines the importance of reclaiming and

125 Owens Patton, 2006.

126 X, Malcolm. 1966. *The Autobiography of Malcolm X*. Compiled by Alex Haley. New York: Grove Press.

127 Craig, Maxine. 1997. "The decline and fall of the conk; or, how to read a process." *Fashion Theory: The Journal of Dress Body, & Culture* 1 (4): 399–419.

celebrating our natural beauty, for it is a crucial part of our cultural heritage and individual identities.[128]

The first wave of the natural-hair movement emerged during the tumultuous 1960s, a time of profound social and political change. During this era, the "Black Is Beautiful" movement arose as a cultural counter-narrative to mainstream beauty standards. This movement assured Black women and men that their skin, facial features, and natural hair were admirable—as is. It was a powerful response to the societal pressures and norms that privileged Eurocentric features and standards.

The activist Marcus Garvey encouraged Black women to embrace their natural kinks, arguing that copying white Eurocentric standards of beauty denigrated the beauty of Black women. "Don't remove the kinks from your hair! Remove them from your brain!"

High-profile activists like Angela Davis, along with many others within the Black community, sported an afro as a sign of Black power and rebellion against white American beauty standards. This hairstyle became emblematic of the wider resistance against oppressive beauty norms. Wearing an afro became a weapon in the fight for racial equality as well as a public declaration of self-love and solidarity within the Black community. Whether rocking afros or pressed hair, Black protesters demanded the signing of the Civil Rights Act of 1964, which "ended segregation in public places and banned employment discrimination." The Act also created the EEOC, which operates "as the lead enforcement agency in the area of workplace discrimination." When the EEOC was founded fifty-five years ago, the federal government's primary concern was that Black people be granted equal access to public workplaces. It didn't foresee that Black people's natural hair would need equal access as well.

128 X, Malcolm, 1966.

The first cases of natural-hair discrimination wouldn't appear until the next decade. In the 1976 case of *Jenkins v. Blue Cross Mutual Hospital Insurance*, the US Court of Appeals for the Seventh Circuit upheld a race discrimination lawsuit against an employer for bias against afros. The appeals court agreed that workers were entitled to wear afros under Title VII of the Civil Rights Act.

While afros were technically allowed in workplaces, the social pressure to emulate Eurocentric hair permeated American society, impacting Black women's hair grooming decisions. The 1980s and 1990s ushered in more Black women sporting pressed and permed hair, reflecting a resurgence of Eurocentric beauty standards. This trend was driven, in part, by prevalent hair-care ads on TV and in magazines that encouraged Black women to alter the texture of their hair. The beauty industry, in reinforcing these norms, exerted a significant influence on societal perceptions of Black hair and identity. However, this time period also witnessed the popularization of styles like braids and cornrows. Images of Black women celebrities showcasing braids—like Janet Jackson in *Poetic Justice*—encouraged Black women to braid their tresses. Wearing these styles came with a price, as they created a legal firestorm. In 1981, a Black woman took American Airlines to court because the company demanded she not wear her hair in braids. The court sided with the airline, stating that braids were not an immutable racial characteristic—unlike the afro. Less than a decade later, the Hyatt Regency used this ruling to make employee Cheryl Tatum resign after she refused to take out the cornrows she wore to work. The American Airlines ruling established a standing legal precedent.[129]

But, despite the legal challenges and implications of relaxed hair, wearing wigs, or using hair weaves to add length or density to our hair, researchers

129   Griffin, Chanté. 2019. "How Natural Black Hair at Work Became a Civil Rights Issue." JSTOR Daily. daily.jstor.org/how-natural-black-hair-at-work-became-a-civil-rights-issue/.

have clarified that straightening one's hair is not synonymous with racial shame or "acting white." In fact, the authors of *Shifting: The Double Lives of Black Women in America*, Charisse Jones and Kumea Shorter-Gooden, argue that "not every woman who decides to straighten her hair or change the color of her eyes by wearing contacts believes that beauty is synonymous with whiteness. Trying on a new look, even one often associated with Europeans, does not automatically imply self-hatred. It is possible to dye your brown tresses platinum and still love your Blackness."[130]

On our *Black Power Moves* podcast, celebrity hair stylist Eugene Davis shared his experiences shaping the hair trends in the music industry during the 1990s. He recalls introducing lace front wigs into the mainstream, a move that led to an industry-wide trend, and collaborating with artists like Lil Kim to create bold, color-coordinated hairstyles. Davis's work, particularly with wigs, contributed to shifting perceptions of Black hair and beauty.

> ...My first assignment was Lil Kim. Before she came out, me and Lil Kim hit it off. And next thing I know, [...] I was doing Biggie Smalls' "One More Chance" video. I had no idea who Biggie Smalls was. I walked in with a whole bunch of hair into his cabin, and he looked at me and he said, "Are you here to do my hair?"
>
> I said, yeah, I got lots of wigs [...] that kind of broke the ice. And of course, "One More Chance" was a video with all the celebrities that were in it. And that was my introduction to Mary, Aaliyah, [...] Changing Faces. So many different artists.
>
> And then from that point on, I was being called and utilized in [...] the music world as a hairstylist. And that's how I got the opportunity to do

130 Jones, Charisse, and Kumea Shorter-Gooden. 2003. *Shifting: The Double Lives of Black Women in America*. New York: HarperCollins Publishers.

protecting my peace

"Crush on You," "Ladies Night" [...] I can't even name. There's so many videos that I did at the time, [...] but the door was wide open.

But that also is how I got a chance to introduce [them] to wigs because at the time, people didn't understand. [...] They were like, "Oh yeah, Grandma wears wigs." I was like, "No." There's lace fronts. And I got introduced to that from watching RuPaul and having a friend take me backstage. And I was looking at it. RuPaul was like, "Oh, look! It just comes up." I was like, "Oh my God! What's that?"

So, then I was told where I could find it. [...] And from that point on, I introduced them to lace fronts. And then the industry got wind of it. And before I knew [it], everybody was doing lace fronts and look at it right now, it is like a hot commodity. But I never claimed at the time that I was one of the pioneers for that because [...] just how I am. I'm not one of those people who say, oh yeah, I started this or I did it first, I'm just not that person.

Black women started to wear these bold colors. It all started with Lil Kim in that video [...] and she was just like, "Okay, you know what? This is what the stages are doing. What can we do that will shock and just make a change in how people view us and our videos?" And that's when we came up with changing the wigs with the backgrounds. [...] And [...] we cut them and we styled them and we put it on me and my team and put it on Lil Kim. And it just became a legendary video.[131]

While stylists like Davis were pushing boundaries in the music industry, a broader cultural shift was taking place. The 2000s welcomed the second wave of the natural-hair movement. Films and the emergence of social media were

131 Eugene, Davis. 2022. "Educating About the Fabric of Hair." Edited by Elizabeth Leiba. In *Black Power Moves*. Spotify. open.spotify.com/episode/5PDEK9BvpcPTk2yt7bt5Xe?si=xWzlAxEoQ7CsRpGeOArxVw.

the movement's catalysts. It fueled a cultural shift that has caused legions of Black women to abandon their perms and pressing combs. YouTube and natural-hair blogs allowed Black women to discuss their hair-care journeys, share hair tutorials, and connect with other women—many of whom were learning to care for their natural hair for the first time. In "YouTube Communities and the Promotion of Natural Hair Acceptance Among Black Women," Cameron Jackson wrote that the social media platform not only enabled newly minted naturalistas to "disseminate information about natural hair" but also caused "a shift in the cultural understanding of natural hair."[132]

Beyond cultural and personal identity, there are health considerations that add another layer to the complex issue of Black hair. In a recent study funded by the US National Institutes of Health, researchers used data from more than 33,000 women taking part in the Sister Study, a large, ongoing study looking for risk factors for breast cancer and other health conditions.

Women enrolled in the study were asked about their use of different kinds of hair products over the previous year, including hair dyes, straighteners, relaxers, and permanents or body waves.

After an average of nearly eleven years of follow-up, women who reported using hair-straightening products were almost twice as likely to have developed uterine cancer as those who did not, after adjusting for other factors that might affect risk. Women who reported frequent use of straighteners (more than four times in the previous year) were about two and a half times more likely to develop uterine cancer.

The researchers did not find links between uterine cancer and the use of other hair products, including hair dyes, highlights, and perms. Data from the Sister Study has been used in the past to look for possible links between

132 Griffin, 2019.

hair products and other cancers, especially cancers that grow in response to hormones. This includes breast and ovarian cancers as well as uterine cancer.

Concerns have been raised about possible links between some hair products and these cancers because some of the chemicals used in hair products might be absorbed through the scalp and have estrogen-like properties in the body. Some hair products might also contain other chemicals that have been linked to cancer, such as formaldehyde. Previous research from the Sister Study has also linked straightener use with a higher risk of breast cancer.

In the current study, about 60 percent of the women who reported using straighteners in the previous year self-identified as being Black. While the study didn't find a difference in the link between straightener use and uterine cancer risk across races, it's important to highlight the potential greater impact on Black women. This disparity stems from the fact that Black women are significantly more likely to use these products, a trend influenced by long-standing societal pressures to conform to Eurocentric beauty standards.[133]

It's important to remember that these hair stories are deeply personal and vary greatly. Like many Black women, I too have gone back and forth between wearing my hair in its natural state, relaxing it, and wearing weaves and wigs. Ultimately, like everything else we do, our hair has become an expression of who we are, rather than defining our racial identity or restricting the choices that we make. Our hair choices should not be limited to natural styles as the only valid form of embracing our identity. I challenge this perspective. Any choice that we willingly make that brings us joy and confidence and allows us to operate at our best is valid. The key is to make these choices for the right reasons and without any associated mental or emotional distress. This

---

133 American Cancer Society, 2022. "Study Finds Possible Link Between Hair Straightening Chemicals and Uterine Cancer." American Cancer Society. www.cancer.org/cancer/latest-news/study-finds-possible-link-between-hair-straightening-chemicals-and-uterine-cancer.htm.

is especially important as we navigate predominantly white spaces where our appearance and identity are often scrutinized. We can make our own choices to determine what our identity means to us.

In conclusion, the journey of Black hair is neither linear nor monolithic. It's a complex, multifaceted account that speaks to our unique identities, our struggles, and our victories. Whether embracing natural textures or experimenting with wigs, weaves, or colors, the essence is that Black women continue to define and redefine their beauty on their own terms. As for me, I'm on my third big chop, and I've never felt more at home with my hair. This freedom to choose and express ourselves is the ultimate form of power.

Despite what society may say or what I see in the media or popular culture, in the words of India Arie, "I am not my hair." I am free to wear it as curly or straight as I want to, and I can love it as much or as little as I want in the ways that I choose or do not, because I define myself. Of course, it would be naive to assert that there would be no pushback from the majority culture about the aesthetics of our hair. "Professionalism," "beauty," and, by extension, the appearance of our hair has never fit the mold, which is why I encourage breaking the mold and leaning on our ancestral tradition of creating our own construct for what beauty means. It's not defined by our skin color—light versus dark—the shape of our lips, the roundness in our hips, or the texture of our hair—kinky and coily versus straight and laid. It emanates from within, and true power and emotional well-being come from embracing ourselves in whatever form we choose to appear, even though we know those choices may not always be accepted or supported in the spaces we inhabit.

Adjoa B. Asamoah, one of the cofounders of the CROWN Coalition, established in early 2019, works toward expanding legal protections for people of color who choose to wear their natural hair without fear of discrimination. When I spoke with her for EBONY Media, Asamoah emphasized the importance of the CROWN Movement: "It's about outlawing race-based hair discrimination... It is acknowledging our racial identity... There is no biological basis for race the way we use it, but that doesn't mean that racism is not very real." She stressed the specific problems race-based hair discrimination creates, from hindering the thriving of our children in school to reinforcing Eurocentric standards that excuse bias in employment and promotions. And she acknowledged the challenges still ahead: "We have a lot of work to continue, but we have been here before. We are cut out to do it. It does not mean that we are not exhausted. We have to remember that rest is part of the movement as well."[134]

The sentiment of rest being part of the movement also echoes Audre Lorde's eloquent statement: "Rest is resistance." Rest means that we shouldn't have to fight against our own natural proclivity for expressing our creativity through the dimensions of our hair. It's a mosaic with all of the beautiful hues of Black, brown, and anything else we choose. It's not necessary for us to sport an afro like Angela Davis to embrace our beautiful Black identity. But we also shouldn't be forced to wear a wig over our natural cornrows because we are afraid of how we will be received. So, we move forward in ways that allow us to embrace the ways we show up that feel good to us. The primary focus should be on our well-being and not on the expectations of others.

Not all of us are on the front lines, fighting for our beauty to be seen, accepted, and even legalized. Yet, we all hold power over how we see ourselves, treat ourselves, and speak to ourselves.

Our emotional balance depends heavily on the way we celebrate our own beauty. It relies on our ability to rest easy in the knowledge of our rich ancestral history and cultural tradition of uplifting our beauty. To be a Black woman is to carry a legacy of resilience, creativity, and strength.

134 Asamoah, Adjoa B. 2022. "Championing the CROWN Act." Edited by Elizabeth Leiba. In *Black Power Moves*. Spotify. open.spotify.com/episode/60CauoZXyQ2Cr7hT4AHDb3.

Our beauty is more than skin deep, and our inability to celebrate it in its full richness can lead to unhealed trauma. But we have the power to turn this around. When I look in the mirror, I no longer rush past my reflection. Instead, I take the time to study the curves of my lips and nose, to appreciate each part of my face that makes me who I am.

Beauty is skin deep, but for Black women, not being able to celebrate our beauty in its full richness can lead to what I describe as "unsealed trauma"—the unresolved emotional wounds that we carry with us. So when I look in the mirror, I've started taking my time to study the curves in my lips and nose. I take the time to acknowledge each part of my face. I note the parts of my face that remind me of my father and the ones that look like my mother. Rather than ruminating about how self-conscious I was about my Black features and natural hair growing up, I take the time to think about how beautifully and wonderfully made I truly am. Everything about me is amazing, and that includes the beauty of my face and full body that radiates from inside.

Celebrating our beauty and creating our own narratives about what that looks like is empowering. It involves understanding how much our confidence and self-esteem as humans rest on how we are perceived and accepted. Yet, as Black women, we face the unique challenge of navigating a world that doesn't necessarily do that.

On the flip side, we are free to uplift each other and ourselves. A casual compliment to a stranger, a "Hey, girl! I love those shoes!" can brighten both her day and ours. I've done it on several occasions and felt the joy when she returns a smiling "Thank you!" It's in these moments that we seize our own narratives of beauty and validation.

Being able to accept compliments is also part of this process. It's a small but significant step in reframing what it means to be beautiful as we walk in society. This reframing is a constant process, a constant assertion that everything about us—from the top of our heads to the soles of our feet—is beautiful without exception.

I still remember being in high school and reading and reciting Maya Angelou's "Phenomenal Woman." The lines, "I'm not cute or built to suit a fashion model's size... Phenomenal woman, that's me," resonate with me even today. The feeling that surges through me when I see another girl who looks like me reciting these lines is transcendent.

I recited this poem, affirming myself in the mirror, and I came to realize the peace that stems from self-acceptance and love. Celebrating my beauty—my fluffy afro, full lips, hips, and nose—became a cherished ritual. It's a practice that has helped me in my journey toward self-acceptance. I am loving myself, and I am giving myself permission to look in the mirror and admire everything I see. A part of this journey to self-acceptance has been uncovering my feelings about myself, not only in my physical form but also in my thoughts and feelings. Unpacking all of these emotions has been instrumental in helping to heal the little girl inside who never had a Black baby doll and, quite frankly, doesn't need one to validate my beauty anymore, because the woman I see looking back at me in the mirror is more than enough!

Learning to love ourselves means that we understand just how much power can be ascribed to our beauty and femininity, which has been counter to the archetype of the strong, asexual Black woman. The Strong Black Woman, Jezebel, and Sapphire are simply archetypes. They are stereotypes used to disempower us, and we can acknowledge them without subscribing to them or acting them out based on society's perception of what it means to be us. We determine that through our own agency. We are in control of our own personal stories, choices, and reactions to what we see around us. I choose the feminine divine because I am a queen. I am the beginning and the end. Once I've accepted that reality, there is no other that affects my existence.

Black women have been viewed as beautiful and a representation of womanhood throughout time. However, most of us are not aware of just how powerful the matriarchal role of Black women has always been. We are aware of how strong mothers and grandmothers were and are. But how much do we know about our ancestral mothers, and how much love, divine wisdom, and contentment flow from how secure they were in every way, and the legacy of well-being that we can draw just from our knowledge of their eternal presence? Part of that process involves focusing on harnessing the beautiful feminine divinity that is a central component of African culture across the diaspora. The love we find there is infinite if we're open to how much peace it can provide.

journaling questions

1. How have societal perceptions and media representation of Black women influenced your own self-image and understanding of beauty?

2. Can you recall specific moments when you felt challenged or empowered by prevailing beauty standards? How did these moments shape your relationship with your self-image?

3. How do you believe the historical oppression of Black women has affected the collective self-image of Black women today?

4. What strategies or approaches do you believe are most effective in combating the negative impact of historical and ongoing oppression on Black women's self-worth and image?

5. How familiar are you with Afrocentric theory, and in what ways might it offer a healing or empowering perspective on self-image?

6. How have you personally experienced or observed colorism within your community, and what steps can be taken to counteract this form of prejudice?

7. How has your community influenced your understanding of beauty and self-worth, both positively and negatively?

8. Considering societal perceptions, media, and historical contexts, what messages would you want to impart to younger Black women to foster a positive self-image?

9. How can sharing personal narratives and stories among Black women help in reshaping the broader narrative around Black beauty and self-image?

10. How do you think intersecting identities, such as sexuality, class, or nationality, further influence the self-image of Black women in the face of societal perceptions and beauty standards?

affirmations

1. I am more than society's portrayal of me; I define my own beauty and worth.

2. Every facet of my being, from the tone of my skin to the texture of my hair, is a testament to a rich heritage and unique beauty.

3. I am the resilient descendant of strong Black women; their strength flows through me, and I carry their legacy with pride.

4. I am an agent of change, and with every step, I challenge the narratives that aim to diminish Black women.

5. By embracing my Afrocentric roots, I ground myself in a rich tapestry of history, culture, and wisdom.

6. I stand against colorism, recognizing the beauty in every shade of Black and advocating for unity in our diversity.

7. Regardless of societal standards, I see my worth, I embrace my beauty, and I celebrate my unique journey.

8. I am on a continual journey of self-love, healing from external judgments and internalized beliefs, and growing in my understanding of self-worth.

9. By sharing my story and listening to the stories of others, I find strength, solidarity, and pathways to collective healing.

10. I am a multifaceted masterpiece, encompassing the beauty, challenges, strengths, and histories of Black womanhood.

Chapter 8

foundations of identity and early influences

"One day I decided that I was beautiful, and so I carried out my life as if I was a beautiful girl. I wear colors that I really like, I wear makeup that makes me feel pretty, and it really helps. It doesn't have anything to do with how the world perceives you. What matters is what you see."

—Gabourey Sidibe

It was the beginning of the fall semester of my junior year, and I was in a panic. Big time! I needed one more class to fill my schedule so I could be considered a full-time student. I needed that status to qualify to stay on scholarship. As a student at the University of Florida in the early '90s, I was the recipient of what at the time was labeled a "minority scholarship award" from the Knight Foundation in Miami, Florida, to increase the number of students from "underrepresented" backgrounds attending school for journalism.

It was the 1990s. All of the discussion around Rodney King, racial equity, and police misconduct, as well as how those incidents were reported in the news, led to a rush to recruit high school students across the country. At my predominantly Black high school in Fort Lauderdale, I had been the editor of my school newspaper, the anchor on the morning news show, and had graduated fifth in a class of two hundred students. However, since arriving on campus, I noticed that the encouragement, nurturing, and guidance I received from teachers, coaches, and mentors was severely lacking.

The high school I attended, Dillard, has a rich history that deeply impacted my education and personal growth. Originally established in 1907 as Colored School Number Eleven, its opening marked the beginning of monumental African American achievement in South Florida. All that time, Fort Lauderdale was a farming region where locals found it unnecessary to educate African Americans past the sixth grade.

Two decades later, the school progressed under principal Dr. Joseph A. Ely, who added more classes and sought to educate African American students past the sixth grade. He was also responsible for the school's current name, a nod to James Harvey Dillard, a white educator from Virginia who was a Black education advocate.

In 1943, at a time when jazz was still a relatively new and rapidly evolving genre, Dillard's well-known jazz program was led by Julius "Cannonball" Adderley.

Adderley would later rise to prominence as one of the best-known jazz musicians in America, and his legacy was a beacon of inspiration throughout my journey at Dillard. Adderley brought new life to the school and helped instill the importance of jazz in the students. He taught jazz when it had not yet been accepted as a classical art form, and while he was teaching jazz, he was also teaching Bach and Beethoven.[135]

Teachers at Dillard never let us forget how great we were and the legacy of greatness we were expected to uphold for the school, our families, and our community. Most of the students were Black, with only around two hundred of the two thousand coming from other ethnic backgrounds. Even though most of us qualified for free and reduced lunch, our teachers schooled us on the riches we couldn't see.[136] Most of our teachers were Black as well, community leaders, involved in politics, and members of Black Greek-letter organizations. No matter our circumstances, they expected nothing but excellence from us. They instilled in us the sense that, regardless of what we had heard or thought, we were the descendants of royalty—Kings and Queens—whether we knew it or not. They expected us to act accordingly. Therefore, we were not permitted to make excuses about the old building, the musty, torn textbooks, or the blood-stained carpet in the hallway resulting from a knife fight where a teacher had his arm sliced in breaking up two girls.

Despite our school's storied past and the challenges we faced, once we stepped into our classrooms, we were encouraged to focus on our education. Here, teachers adorned in kente cloth and black medallions guided us, and we expressed ourselves freely, often rapping and beating on desks before class. Our sing-song voices reverberated through the hallways, and everything about

135 Henry, Carma. 2016. "Dillard High School continues to make history!" The Westside Gazette, June 23, 2016. thewestsidegazette.com/dillard-high-school-continues-to-make-history/.

136 "Search for Public Schools—DILLARD 6–12 (120018000169)." 2022. NCES. nces.ed.gov/ccd/schoolsearch/school_detail. asp?Search=1&DistrictID=1200180&SchoolPageNum=8&ID=120018000169.

us was celebrated because everyone who came into contact with us wanted us to win. It was there that I was introduced to *African Origins of Civilization* by Chiek Anta Diop and *The Isis Papers* by Dr. Frances Cress Welsing, and I started to wonder about the untapped power inside my body.

My eleventh-grade African American studies teacher was the man who had his arm sliced. On the first day of class, he excitedly passed out copies of *The Miseducation of the Negro* by Carter G. Woodson. He had bought them himself, unpacking them carefully from a brown carton and handing one to each of us. He warned us to read it and understand it because we would be discussing the concepts in class. The sleeves of his button-down shirt were rolled up slightly. We could see the knife scar on his arm, and we whispered about it to each other. Why did he stay? Why was he still here at this dilapidated school? We knew it wasn't for the money. Teachers always complained that they didn't make enough. He never did! He was involved in local politics, a member of Kappa Alpha Psi Fraternity, Inc., and had owned a barber shop for years in the neighborhood not far from our school.

His actions spoke louder than his words: he spent countless hours after school tutoring us, organized field trips to expose us to the world beyond our neighborhood, and always had an open ear for anyone who needed to talk. He was there for us, no doubt, and his every action was a testament to his words that he loved everything about us and would do anything in his power to ensure we knew the truth of our identities. One day, he brought in a book brimming with African names and their meanings. He passed it around, inviting each of us to select a name that would be our identifier in his class. When we walked into class, that was the name he would call us. Everyone else in the class was instructed to do the same. When the book was passed to me, I flipped through the pages and selected one of the first names I saw. It spoke to me.

Amina: Trustworthy, faithful (ah-MEE-nah—Arabic, North Africa; Swahili, East Africa). Amen (Mende, West Africa). Popular name with the Hausa people of West Africa. Form of Aminah, the name of Muhammad's mother: peaceful, secure (Arabic, North Africa).[137]

I stared at that entry for a few minutes before telling him my selection. "Alright, Amina!" he confirmed with a smile. I smiled back shyly, glad that he approved, and handed the book to the student sitting at the desk behind me. Each face in the classroom was turned toward us. Each student anxiously awaited his or her turn to choose the African name that would define them in this classroom. I savored the meaning of my new name along with everything else he suggested—for us to empower ourselves by reading about our African history and culture. My whole mind frame shifted within the months that I took this brand-new elective that had been rolled out because this teacher had pushed the administration to offer us this gift—an opportunity to learn who we really were.

I have to admit that up until that point, I had been conflicted. And I had thought about it quite a lot. Who was I? In theory, I was a young Black woman growing up on the predominantly Black eastside of Fort Lauderdale. But I was also an immigrant, born in the United Kingdom in London. My parents had been raised in London, but both arrived there as teenagers after spending their formative years in Jamaica. My Dad's side of the family proudly embraced their Cuban roots, but none of us actually spoke Spanish. This was much to the chagrin of Spanish speakers I met, who were everywhere I turned in South Florida and recognized the origins of my last name.

Despite the empowering environment within my school, once I stepped outside its gates, I found myself surrounded by an environment that often left me feeling lost and confused. In this environment, amidst the chaos and the questions, I found myself grappling with a harsh reality. The poverty

---

137 Keister, Linda W. n.d. "Amina." The Black Names Project. Accessed July 3, 2023. www.blacknamesproject.com/node/163.

of our neighborhoods, the unfamiliarity with the African experience in America—it was like standing on the threshold of two different worlds, a personal microcosm of the larger societal issues I would later dedicate myself to understanding and challenging. I asked myself why my only frame of reference was a television show called *Roots* that I had watched as a child in London. Why was everyone at my school Black? Coming from a primary school in southeast London, where I had been one of only three Black students, this was a real culture shock. Now my teacher was waving this book by Carter G. Woodson as he stood at the front of the class, telling us there was so much more to our story than *Roots*. What did he mean? Why were the only white kids who attended bussed in for the Performing Arts Magnet program? Why did they take classes in a totally separate building? There were so many questions that needed to be answered. But the one answer that my teachers continued to reinforce was a question I hadn't asked. They told me I was royalty. They told me my ancestors built the pyramids. They told me they expected the world from me. They told me I was a queen.

Our classrooms were spaces where we not only learned about who we really were, but also where our teachers, often better than many of our parents, nurtured us. Many of our parents were immigrants going back to school, or had low-paying jobs. Some worked more than one job to pay the bills. Their form of encouragement usually involved stern talks to let us know that reports from teachers about our misconduct in class wouldn't be tolerated.

We knew we had to pay attention to the teachers because they admonished us emphatically to ignore all of the background noise, including the depressing neighborhood filled with aging homes, the fact that our parents had to work two jobs to keep a roof over our heads, the poor test results, and the books that were falling apart. None of that mattered. We were told to hold our heads high and not make excuses.

My American History teacher had made that fact abundantly clear the year before. She was a member of Alpha Kappa Alpha Sorority, Inc., and had zero tolerance for excuses. In fact, on the first day of class, she gave us one assignment. If we completed it correctly without any mistakes, we received a perfect score of 100 percent. Any mistakes would earn us a zero. We were to go to the podium at the front of the class. She had us recite a mantra that became our rallying cry against mediocrity: "Excuses are tools of incompetence used to build bridges to nowhere and monuments of nothingness, and those who use them seldom specialize in anything else." This mantra, she explained, was a call for us to take responsibility and strive for excellence in all we did.

Of course, I got a perfect score! My high school years shaped me significantly, and I graduated fifth in my class. However, as I transitioned to the University of Florida, I found myself missing the nurturing teachers and personally invested role models I had grown accustomed to at Dillard. I was on a campus where few looked like me, and most people I encountered looked through me as though I didn't even exist. I was an inconvenience who didn't belong there. The fact that I was there on a minority scholarship was all the "proof" they needed that I had taken a spot that I didn't deserve, at least not in their blue, green, and hazel eyes. It was the early 1990s, and even though Black people represented 13.6 percent of Florida's population, only 5 percent of the school's almost 27,000 students were Black.[138]

In my freshman year, I was drawn to one particular professor, the only Black professor I had that year. He taught Introduction to African American Studies, a class fondly referred to as AFA 2000, and was a beacon of understanding and guidance for all the Black students on campus, including me. This class was a shared experience; every Black student had taken it at

---

138   *Sun Sentinel.* 1992. "WHITE UNIVERSITIES FAILING TO SATISFY BLACK STUDENTS." November 29, 1992. www.sun-sentinel.com/1992/11/29/white-universities-failing-to-satisfy-black-students/.

some point during their time there. His name was Dr. Ronald C. Foreman, Jr. He had earned his BA degree from Hampton University, a historically Black college in Hampton, VA, in 1949, and a master's in English from another HBCU, North Carolina Central University, in Durham, NC, in 1950. Finally, he had a PhD in mass communications from the University of Illinois.

Prior to teaching at the University of Florida, Dr. Foreman taught at a number of historically Black schools in the South, including Shaw University, Knoxville College, and Tuskegee University. Subsequently, he was hired by the University of Florida in 1970, where he was among the first group of tenure-track Black faculty members to be hired. At UF, he served as the first director of the African American Studies department, a position he held until his retirement in 2000.

He had a special interest in the origins of African American blues and jazz music, an interest that became a core component of the curriculum he taught the many students who took his AFA 2000 class at UF during his thirty-year teaching career.[139]

He was soft-spoken and thoughtful. He always took his time to fully answer any question we asked during his class. He was the only professor I confided in when I was falsely accused of shoplifting and arrested my sophomore year after being racially profiled in a local pharmacy. He listened sympathetically, without any judgment, and encouraged me to stay strong, reminding me of the history and legacy that were a part of what I was experiencing. I had filed a civil lawsuit against the company that had had me arrested, even though I had a receipt for the two-dollar item they accused me of stealing.

139 "Ronald Foreman Obituary (2014)—Gainesville, FL—Gainesville Sun." 2014. Legacy.com. www.legacy.com/us/obituaries/gainesville/name/ronald-foreman-obituary?id=16636358.

In his class, all young men were required to remove their hats. He explained the importance he had learned growing up in the South of removing his hat when ladies were present. He was always sure to carefully remove his plaid, snap-front newsboy cap whenever he entered the classroom. He expected us to be on time for class. He asked that we be ready to discuss the books he reminded us were required reading for his class: *The Souls of Black Folk* by W.E.B. DuBois, *Up From Slavery* by Booker T. Washington, *Makes Me Wanna Holler* by Nathan McCall, and *The Color of Water* by James McBride. I read each one voraciously, feeding the appetite that had been awakened during my high school years. I needed to know everything about myself, and this was just one more pathway to understanding.

And the conundrum I faced during the spring semester of my junior year seemed to have a solution very much in line with my hunger for knowledge. I needed just one more class to meet my full-time enrollment requirement. It was a condition for maintaining my scholarship, which was not just an award for me but a lifeline that kept my academic dreams alive. I frantically searched through the schedule of open classes haphazardly posted with Scotch Tape at the reception desk in my college dorm. Wait! There was a class that caught my eye!

AFS 4335: Women in Africa
Explores issues of gender, development, and culture through memoirs, ethnographies, narratives, and films about women in Africa.

This was exactly what I needed to complete my bare minimum of twelve hours to be a full-time student while learning all about women in precolonial Africa. Sounded interesting... And even better, there were only a handful of students currently enrolled. I was in there, like swimwear!

But the first day was a huge disappointment. At the front of the classroom stood a petite, white lady with a blunt-cut bob of salt and pepper hair. I had anticipated learning about African history and women from someone who shared the same roots and experiences, and her presence initially struck a dissonant note. She was dressed in a plaid skirt, sensible low-heeled shoes, and a brown cardigan. "Where is her kente cloth?" I hesitated at the entrance of the small, brightly lit room and quickly glanced at my schedule and the room number to make sure I was in the right place. I was. "Hmmmm... Okay..." I thought to myself, sliding into a seat in the front of the class. I slumped over, reading the school newspaper and reviewing the syllabus, while I skeptically waited for her to begin the lecture. What I would learn from this woman over the next sixteen weeks of the semester changed not only the way I perceived the African diaspora, but specifically how I viewed myself as a Black person and a Black woman.

journaling questions

1. Reflecting on your African ancestry, how do your forebears' stories, struggles, and triumphs contribute to your understanding of self and your place in the world?

2. How does gaining knowledge of Black women's pivotal roles throughout history influence your sense of pride, worth, and capability in today's society?

3. How do the diverse cultures, traditions, and values from African societies shape your worldview and personal identity? Are there specific cultural practices or traditions that resonate deeply with you?

4. Think of a mentor or role model from the Black community who has significantly impacted your life. How have their guidance and wisdom shaped your personal and professional journey?

5. How can you actively contribute to ensuring the younger generation in the Black community receives the mentorship, encouragement, and nurturing they need to thrive? What roles can you play in fostering such environments?

6. How does embracing your African ancestry and the rich history of Black women empower you to face challenges and navigate spaces where your identity might be marginalized or misunderstood?

7. How does understanding and celebrating your Black heritage contribute to your mental health, emotional well-being, and overall sense of purpose?

8. Why do you think it's essential for the younger generation in the Black community to be well-versed in their history and culture? How can you contribute to this education and cultural transmission?

9. How can connecting deeply with your African roots and the shared history of Black women create a stronger sense of unity and solidarity within the community?

10. As you reflect on your journey and the importance of African ancestry in forming a positive identity, what legacy do you wish to leave for the younger generation? How do you envision them carrying the torch forward, understanding their roots, and shaping the future?

affirmations

1. I am deeply rooted in the rich tapestry of African history; its stories of strength and resilience shape my identity and drive my purpose.

2. My African ancestry empowers me, reminding me daily of the strength, wisdom, and resilience that flows through my veins.

3. I am a continuation of a powerful legacy of Black women leaders, thinkers, and creators; I honor their struggles by thriving and uplifting others.

4. Through the mentorship of the trailblazing Black women before me, I find guidance, wisdom, and inspiration to navigate my path.

5. I am committed to nurturing, guiding, and mentoring the younger generation, ensuring they recognize the greatness within them and the potential they possess.

6. By immersing myself in Black history and culture, I fortify my spirit, boost my confidence, and find a wellspring of wisdom to draw from.

7. In embracing my true self and celebrating my African roots, I find an unmatched strength, confidence, and a deep sense of belonging.

8. Every day I affirm that my identity, grounded in my African ancestry, is a source of pride, strength, and unwavering resilience.

9. I am a beacon of hope and strength for my community, reminding them of our shared history, our potential, and the bright future we can create together.

10. Understanding and celebrating my Black heritage nourishes my soul, fortifies my mental well-being, and fills me with a purposeful joy.

the African sacred feminine and historical stereotyping

"I think any black woman is a queen.
It's just, do you know it? Do you see it in yourself?"

—Ava DuVernay

In the heart of Africa, where the dawn of civilization and culture is as vast as the sun-scorched savannahs, lies the ethos of the African Sacred Feminine. A lineage of strength, resilience, and infinite wisdom, this powerful archetype stands in stark contrast to the often one-dimensional narrative projected upon Black women today. In this realm of ancestral memories, the Black woman was revered, not just as a nurturer but as a force of creation, leadership, and transformation.

The African Sacred Feminine is not just an archaic ideal. For the modern Black woman, it represents a deep reservoir of empowerment and identity, a vivid counter-narrative to prevalent stereotypes. Today, she is often caught in the crossfire of societal perceptions, which box her into restrictive roles—the sassy friend, the Angry Black Woman, the oversexualized object. Such stereotypes do not merely remain on the screens; they permeate real lives, limiting opportunities and dictating interactions.

But why should the modern Black woman, sophisticated and urbane, turn her gaze back to a mythic past? Simply put, because within the Sacred Feminine lies a truth so profound that it transcends time and place. By embracing these ideals, Black women tap into an empowering narrative that has been obscured but never obliterated. This Sacred Feminine is the matriarch that led communities, the queen that ruled empires, the priestess that connected the earthly with the divine. This narrative tells the Black woman that she is not just a caricature born of modern prejudices, but the heiress of a rich legacy, pulsating with the rhythms of Africa.

Societal perceptions are not just limiting; they are damaging. When Black women are continuously shown as aggressive or hypersexual, it is not merely an image issue—it lays the groundwork for systemic discrimination. These perceptions affect opportunities for employment, interactions with law enforcement, and even access to healthcare. By anchoring herself in the strength of the African Sacred Feminine, the Black woman can counteract the weight of these stereotypes, challenging them with a history and spirituality that speaks of her true essence.

However, this isn't a journey of mere rediscovery; it is a continuous process of decolonizing the mind. Centuries of colonial and post-colonial narratives have shaped perceptions of Black womanhood. Unraveling these threads is not the work of a day or a year. It is a lifelong commitment to challenge, question, and redefine. Every Black woman, whether she's in the bustling streets of Lagos or the sprawling avenues of New York, carries within her the echoes of the Sacred Feminine. Listening to these echoes, allowing them to shape her identity and worldview, is the process of decolonization.

This journey is poetic, for it involves a dance with the past, a song of self-affirmation, and a continuous crafting of one's narrative. It is analytical, as it involves the critical examination of accepted norms and the deconstruction of harmful stereotypes. In the Sacred Feminine, the modern Black woman finds not just a symbol, but a beacon—guiding her toward a future where she is defined not by societal prejudices, but by the strength, wisdom, and grace that have always been her heritage.

Although contemporary US society is full of stereotypical images that marginalize and degrade Black women's bodies,[140] many precolonial, spiritually-based cultures of North and West Africa[141] developed indigenous concepts of the African Sacred Feminine. It's a term Arisika Razak, Professor Emerita and former chair of the Women's Spirituality Program at the California Institute of Integral Studies, uses to describe African representations of the feminine aspects of nature and divinity, as well as the innate human and spiritual powers embodied by women.

---

140 Hill Collins, Patricia. 2009. *Black Feminist Thought: Knowledge, Consciousness, and the Politics of Empowerment.* New York: Routledge.

141 Badejo, Diedre. 1996. *Osun Seegesi: The Elegant Deity of Wealth, Power, and Femininity.* Trenton: Africa World Press.

protecting my peace

Many Black women in the United States still find themselves oppressed by Eurocentric beauty standards, patriarchal gender norms, and racist depictions of Black female sexuality that identify Black women as "sexual deviants."[142] Prominent Black authors like bell hooks and Toni Morrison have explored the degrading stereotypes of Black women that arose in the aftermath of the transatlantic slave trade. They dissect how caricatures of self-effacing mammies, lascivious breeders, and tragic mulattoes were crafted and proliferated, extending their influence into the Jim Crow era and beyond. These negative social constructs have been repackaged for modern consumption in the twentieth and twenty-first centuries. Now, they surface in forms like the oversexualized depictions of Black women in media, or the stereotype of the "Angry Black Woman," which are used to police, critique, and marginalize Black women today. In contrast to this historical linking of Black physiognomy with negative, genetically inherited human (or subhuman) traits,[143] the approach of the African Sacred Feminine is to espouse, uplift, and amplify images of African women developed by a variety of historic African cultures, several of which existed millennia before the transatlantic slave trade and the development of modern racism.[144]

In the fifteenth century, a layman, Hans Vintler, began a campaign to taint the positive image of Black female royalty by claiming that "King Solomon had lost his mind because of a Black temptress." His text was accompanied by an illustration, *Die Blumend der Tugend*, showing Solomon worshiping an idol. A Black woman with flowing hair and a deviant glare is positioned in front of him to indicate that she, not he, is guilty of luring Solomon to such "ungodly" worship.

142 Hill Collins, Patricia. 2013. *On Intellectual Activism*. Philadelphia: Temple University Press.

143 Drake, St. Clair. *Black Folk Here and There: An Essay in History and Anthropology*. United States: Center for Afro-American Studies, University of California, 1987.

144 Razak, Ariska. 2016. "Sacred Women of Africa and the African Diaspora: A Womanist Vision of Black W Vision of Black Women's Bodies and the African Sacr s Bodies and the African Sacred Feminine." *International Journal of Transpersonal Studies* 35 (1): 129–147.

Vintler's accusatory contribution was a disaster for the heritage of African womanhood in the West. Afterwards, negative symbolism became increasingly attached to women of African heritage. By the late fifteenth century, vicious racist stereotypes had taken hold—stigmas of hypersexuality, savagery, and intellectual inferiority, among others. These stereotypes persist in various forms even today, influencing social attitudes, systemic bias, and the lived experiences of Black people.[145]

According to Meisenhelder, sixteenth-century writings still stressed how different, culturally and sometimes even physically, Africans were from Europeans. Africans (e.g., the Hottentots) were often believed to be the most primitive of all human beings. The African other was constituted as possessing a human body, mind, and soul, but its body was less evolved, with a skin that was black, a mind that was primitive, and a soul darkened by sin.

Distorted perceptions cast Africans as brutes, supposedly ruled by bodily passion, in stark contrast to the observers' ideal of Christian discipline—a gross misrepresentation revealing more about their own bias than the reality of African culture. Europeans came to perceive Africans through a skewed lens, labeling them as primitive and attributing a range of misrepresented practices to them, from polygamy and heightened sexuality to human sacrifice and cannibalism, casting their spiritual traditions as "paganism." Detailed descriptions of Africans' physical attributes, often laden with racial bias and misinterpretation, played a crucial role in this process of social construction. Exaggerated features and misrepresented characteristics were seized upon, fostering stereotypes and forming the bedrock of long-lasting racial prejudices. Regardless of the array of ways Africans might be perceived, there was an undue emphasis on their skin color, with their Blackness often being the first characteristic noted and, unfortunately, judged upon. Africans were misperceived as being more "natural" and somehow less intellectual, an inaccurate stereotype

---

145 Salami, 2015.

that presented a stark dichotomy: they could be great and beautiful warriors, but they were also regarded as having simple and primitive minds.[146]

The objectification of Black women's bodies in particular abounds in tragic examples, such as the short life of Sarah Baartman, a Khoikhoi woman who was exhibited as a freak-show attraction in nineteenth-century Europe under the name "Hottentot Venus," a name that was later attributed to at least one other woman similarly exhibited. The women were exhibited for their "steatopygia" body type, defined by an accumulation of a large amount of fat on the buttocks. This was uncommon in Western Europe and was not only perceived as a curiosity at that time, but also became the subject of scientific interest as well as erotic projection.

"Venus" is sometimes used to designate representations of the female body in arts and cultural anthropology, referring to the Roman goddess of love and fertility. "Hottentot" was a colonial-era term for the indigenous Khoikhoi people of southwestern Africa, now usually considered an offensive term. The Sarah Baartman story is often regarded as the epitome of racist colonial exploitation and the commodification of the dehumanization of Black people.[147]

Sarah Baartman was a South African woman of Khoikhoi descent, born around 1789. She became a symbol of the deep-seated racism and objectification that Black women have endured historically and continue to face today.

Baartman was lured from her home under the pretext of wealth and fame and brought to Europe, where she was showcased as a spectacle in early nineteenth-century freak shows. Her body, particularly her large buttocks and labia, became objects of fascination, ridicule, and scientific inquiry among Europeans who viewed her as an exotic other. When she died in 1815, her body was dissected and displayed in a Paris museum until 1974, further dehumanizing her posthumously.

---

146 Meisenhelder, 2003.

147 Parkinson, Justin. 2016. "The significance of Sarah Baartman." BBC. www.bbc.com/news/magazine-35240987.

The story of Sarah Baartman symbolizes the hypersexualization and objectification of Black women's bodies, which have been historically reduced to mere spectacles for the male gaze. The use of her body for entertainment and scientific inquiry mirrors the broader historical context where Black bodies were used as objects in the slave trade and medical experiments.

Sarah Baartman's life, exploitation, and public display, even in death, exemplify the racialized and gendered gaze that reduces Black women to their bodies and denies them their full humanity. Her story symbolizes the racist and sexist attitudes deeply rooted in Western society that continue to affect the lives of Black women today.

In today's society, the echoes of Baartman's story reverberate in the way Black women's bodies continue to be exoticized and stereotyped. We see this reflected in many realms: media representation often focuses on certain physical features of Black women, like the trend of non-Black celebrities emulating fuller lips and curvier bodies; social media influencers are regularly accused of "Blackfishing" or altering their appearance to look Black; and in advertising, where Black women's bodies are often depicted in a hypersexualized or objectified manner. The legacy of this harmful practice manifests in the continued commodification of Black women's bodies in media and popular culture, their over-sexualization in music videos, and even the perpetuation of beauty standards that devalue Black features while simultaneously appropriating them.

In deconstructing the harmful legacy of the objectification of Black women, Sarah Baartman's story plays a vital role. She has become a symbol of resistance and a catalyst for dialogue about the ongoing dehumanization of Black women. Her posthumous repatriation to South Africa in 2002 and the subsequent removal of her remains from public display were symbolic acts of justice and resistance against her objectification.

The retelling of Baartman's story also serves as a reminder of the insidious ways in which the legacy of racism and sexism persists. It sparks discussions about how society values and perceives Black women and how these perceptions contribute to systemic racism and sexism. As a symbol, Baartman compels us to challenge and dismantle these harmful portrayals and practices, calling for a more respectful and inclusive recognition of Black women's humanity. In the face of ongoing struggles, the memory of Sarah Baartman serves as a beacon of resistance against objectification and dehumanization.

Sarah Baartman's story deserves to be told. In telling her story, I honor her courage to endure and her resilience under the most horrific of circumstances, and I continue to uncover and share the truth about how Black women's bodies have been treated, not only in the past but with repercussions for all of us in the present day. There is nothing new under the sun. And the goal of understanding the nature of our history ensures that we don't fall victim to the trauma-inducing gaslighting. It happens when Black women go into the world, whether in the boardrooms of corporate America or the local grocery store. The idea that a fixation on our bodies is all in our minds needs to end. Armed with the truth, our ability to distinguish fact from fiction is an integral part of our healing journey. None of this is in our imagination, because it has been happening since our first encounters with colonizers in our native land.

The tragedy of Sarah Baartman is not unique. Documented cases abound that show similar exploitation and objectification of the Black female body, perpetuating a stereotype that seeks to "other" us in body, spirit, and mind. These types of stereotypes run directly counter to the cultural tradition and philosophy of adoration, respect, and appreciation shown to the African woman in her fully glorious form. It's important to understand that the purpose of a stereotype is simplification. The Oxford English Dictionary defines a stereotype as "a widely held but fixed and oversimplified image or idea of a particular type of person or thing."[148] So, beyond the damage wrought by the racist, sexist, and misogynistic purposes of these types of archetypes, they also seek to paint Black women as one-dimensional and lacking

148 "Stereotype." n.d. Oxford Reference. Accessed July 5, 2023. www.oxfordreference.com/display/10.1093/oi/ authority.20110803100530532;jsessionid=022F8C533615C62CE4CE90B41DF2AA17.

in depth, dimension, and complexity. Keeping this in mind provides a perspective to better understand these images, innuendos, stories, and outright lies. Although it can be emotionally taxing to process such damaging portrayals, it is crucial to remember that these stereotypes are not reflective of the rich complexity and diversity of Black womanhood. By engaging in self-care practices, seeking supportive communities, and celebrating the true breadth of Black women's experiences and identities, we can resist internalizing these harmful representations. These stereotypes can be objectively viewed for what they are—a smear campaign to create a false ideal about Black women. The end.

The following stereotypes are examples of the nefarious ways in which the majority culture seeks to further marginalize and emotionally damage Black women. These women have always served as the foundation of the Black family. By objectifying Black women, the goal has always been to destabilize the Black family and further drive a wedge between Black men and Black women, who, throughout antiquity and beyond to the present day, have always been unstoppable when united.

Mammy

The Mammy archetype described enslaved Black women who worked in the houses of plantation owners, often serving as nannies and providing maternal care to the white children of the family. They were characterized as receiving an unusual degree of trust and affection from their enslavers. Early accounts of the Mammy archetype come from memoirs and diaries that emerged after the American Civil War, idealizing the role of the dominant female "house slave": a woman completely dedicated to the white family, especially the children, and given complete charge of domestic management. She was a "friend" and "advisor."[149]

~~~~~~~~~

149   White, Deborah G. 1999. *Ar'n't I a woman?: female slaves in the plantation South.* New York: WW Norton.

Sapphire

The Sapphire stereotype is of a domineering Black female who consumes men and usurps their role, characterized as a strong, masculine workhorse who labored with Black men in the fields, or an aggressive woman whose overbearing drove away her children and partners.[150] Her assertive demeanor is similar to "the Mammy." But she is portrayed as lacking maternal compassion and understanding.

Jezebel

Jezebel is a stereotype of a sexually voracious, promiscuous Black woman, and was the counterimage of the demure Victorian lady.[151] The idea stemmed from Europeans' first encounters with seminude women in tropical Africa. The African practice of polygamy was attributed to uncontrolled lust, and tribal dances were construed as pagan orgies. These traditional cultural practices were juxtaposed with the European Christian notion of chastity.

Content warning: sexual violence. During the era of slavery, degrading stereotypes about Black women's sexuality were employed to legitimize abhorrent actions taken by enslavers, including forced reproduction and sexual violence. These stereotypes even found their way into the legal system, further perpetuating harm against Black women.[152] Because white people claimed that

150 Jerald, Morgan C., L. M. Ward, Kyla D. Fletcher, Lolita Moss, Khia Thomas, and Kyla D. Fletcher. 2017. "Subordinates, Sex Objects, or Sapphires? Investigating Contributions of Media Use to Black Students' Femininity Ideologies and Stereotypes About Black Women." *Journal of Black Psychology* 43, no. 6 (September): 608–635.

151 Anderson, Joel R., Elise Holland, Courtney Heldreth, and Scott P. Johnson. 2018. "Revisiting the Jezebel Stereotype: The Impact of Target Race on Sexual Objectification." *Psychology of Women Quarterly* 42, no. 4 (December): 461–476.

152 Leath, Seanna, Martinque Jones, Morgan C. Jerald, and Tiani R. Perkins. 2022. "An investigation of Jezebel stereotype awareness, gendered racial identity and sexual beliefs and behaviors among Black adult women." *Culture, Health & Sexuality* 24, no. 4 (April): 517–532.

Black women always wanted sex, it was impossible to prove that they were rape victims in court.[153] The Jezebel stereotype contrasts with the Mammy stereotype, providing two broad categories for pigeonholing Black women among whites.[154]

Tragic Mulatta

A stereotype that was popular in early Hollywood, the "tragic mulatta," served as a cautionary tale for Black people. She was usually depicted as a sexually attractive, light-skinned woman who was of African descent but could pass for Caucasian.[155] The stereotype portrayed light-skinned women as obsessed with getting ahead, with their ultimate goal being marriage to a white, middle-class man. The only route to redemption would be for her to accept her "Blackness."

Strong Black Woman

The "Strong Black Woman" trope is a discourse on morality, self-help, economic empowerment, and assimilative values in the greater interest of racial uplift and pride.[156] In this portrait, originating in the Black Baptist church and evolving into a greater popular culture and media archetype, historians have documented the attempts of middle-class Black women to push back against dominant racist portrayals of Black women being immoral, promiscuous, unclean, lazy, and mannerless by engaging in public outreach campaigns that include literature

153 Washington, Patricia A. 2001. "Disclosure Patterns of Black Female Sexual Assault Survivors." *Violence Against Women 7*, no. 11 (November): 1254–1283.

154 Donovan, Roxanne A. 2011. "Tough or Tender: (Dis)Similarities in White College Students' Perceptions of Black and White Women." *Psychology of Women Quarterly 35*, no. 3 (September): 458–468.

155 Bost, Suzanne. 1998. "Fluidity without Postmodernism: Michelle Cliff and the "Tragic Mulatta" Tradition." *African American Review 32* (4): 673–689.

156 Higginbotham, Evelyn B. 1993. *Righteous Discontent: The Women's Movement in the Black Baptist Church, 1880–1920.* Edited by Evelyn B. Higginbotham. Cambridge: Harvard University Press.

that warns against brightly colored clothing, gum chewing, loud talking, and unclean homes, among other directives.[157] This discourse has been shown to be harmful, dehumanizing, and isolating, creating a culture of emotional disconnect and encouraging the festering of racial trauma both inside and outside the Black community.

The "Strong Black Woman" stereotype is a controlling image that perpetuates the idea that it is acceptable to mistreat Black women because we are strong and can handle it. This storyline can also act as a silencing method. When Black women are struggling to be heard because they go through things in life like everyone else, others remind them that they are strong instead of taking actions toward alleviating their challenges and making spaces emotionally safe.[158]

Welfare Queen

The Welfare Queen stereotype depicts a Black woman who defrauds the public welfare system to support herself, having roots in both race and gender. This stereotype negatively portrays Black women as scheming and lazy, ignoring the statistically proven, historically verified, and systemically perpetuated genuine economic hardships that Black women, especially mothers, disproportionately face.[159]

157 Corbin, Nichola, William Smith, and Roberto J. Garcia. 2018. "Trapped between justified anger and being the strong Black woman: Black college women coping with racial battle fatigue at historically and predominantly White institutions." *International Journal of Qualitative Studies in Education* 31, no. 7 (May): 626.

158 Corbin, et al., 2018.

159 Woodard, Jennifer B., and Teresa Mastin. 2005. "Black Womanhood: Essence and its Treatment of Stereotypical Images of Black Women." *Journal of Black Studies* 36, no. 2 (November): 264–281.

Angry Black Woman

In the twenty-first century, the "Angry Black Woman" has evolved into a stereotype depicting Black women as loud, aggressive, demanding, uncivilized, and physically threatening, as well as lower-middle-class and materialistic.[160] She will not stay in what is perceived as her "proper" place.[161]

Controlling images are stereotypes that are used against marginalized groups to portray social injustice as natural, normal, and inevitable. These images serve to erase individuality, silencing Black women and rendering them invisible within society. One misleading aspect of these controlling images is the erroneous suggestion that white women serve as the standard for all aspects of life, even when it comes to understanding oppression.[162] By erasing Black women's individuality, controlling images silence them and render them invisible in society.[163] The assumption that white women are the standard for everything including oppression overlooks the unique ways in which Black women encounter intersectional oppression, which combines race and gender and is not adequately captured by comparing it to the experiences of white women.[164]

Studies demonstrate that white men and women have dominated the field of scholarship on these issues. Being a recognized academic includes social activism as well as scholarship. Scholars note that it is notably difficult for a Black woman to

160 Harris-Perry, Melissa V. 2011. *Sister Citizen: Shame, Stereotypes, and Black Women in America.* London: Yale University Press.

161 Jones, Trina, and Kimberly Norwood. 2017. "Aggressive Encounters & White Fragility: Deconstructing the Trope of the Angry Black Woman." *Iowa Law Review* 102 (5).

162 Collins, 2009.

163 Harris-Perry, 2011.

164 Jones and Norwood, 2017.

receive the resources needed to complete her research and to write the texts that she desires.[165] That, in part, is due to the silencing effect of the "Angry Black Woman" stereotype. Black women are skeptical of raising issues—also seen as complaining— in professional settings because of their fear of being judged.[166] For those of us who pursue social justice advocacy, we often find our experiences minimized and marginalized. We are relegated to living under the broad umbrella of inclusivity or emotional well-being without the context of race in America to frame exactly how centrally impactful the dynamic is to our overall mental health. That is a difficult position to hold, since white counterparts dominate the activist and social work realms of scholarship, reducing scholarship to cookie-cutter solutions without a focus on the voices of Black women, who need advocacy and relief from the pressures of a society dominated by viewpoints centering those in the majority.

Due to the Angry Black Woman stereotype, Black women tend to become desensitized to their own feelings to avoid judgment. They often feel that they must show no emotion outside of their comfortable spaces. That results in the accumulation of these feelings of hurt, which can be projected on loved ones as anger. Once seen as angry, Black women are always seen in that light, and their opinions, aspirations, and values are dismissed.[167] The repression of those feelings can also result in serious mental health issues, which creates a complex for the Strong Black Woman. As a common problem within the Black community, Black women seldom seek help for their mental health challenges.[168]

In a recent *Forbes* article, author and diversity, equity and inclusion consultant Dr. Janice Gassam Asare further explains the harm being done to Black women as we endure the onslaught of trauma from being exposed

165 Griffin, Rachel A., "I AM an Angry Black Woman: Black Feminist Autoethnography, Voice, and Resistance."

166 Harris-Perry, 2011.

167 Beauboeuf-Lafontant, Tamara. 2009. *Behind the Mask of the Strong Black Woman: Voice and the Embodiment of a Costly Performance.* Philadelphia: Temple University Press.

168 Ward, Earlise C., Leondra Clark, and Susan Heidrich. 2009. "African American Women's Beliefs, Coping Behaviors, and Barriers to Seeking Mental Health Services." *Qualitative Health Research* 19, no. 11 (November): 1589–1601.

daily to these negative stereotypes and facing the effects of, not only how we navigate the predominantly white spaces we inhabit, but also how we are perceived and received in those spaces. The results are at once illuminating, revealing, and frankly exhausting to fully grasp. It's helpful to first revisit the difficult situation that Black women in particular face in order to frame these discussions and the process of understanding the results, using the negative effects of misogyny or intersectionality that Kimberlé Crenshaw first identified in 1989. She identifies how race, class, gender, and other intersecting systems shape the experiences of many, perpetuating privilege. Crenshaw used intersectionality to display the disadvantages caused by intersecting systems creating structural, political, and representational aspects of violence against minorities in the workplace and society.[169]

Dr. Asare explains that, when trying to understand a person's experiences, intersectionality is an important consideration. Intersectionality was initially defined as the unique forms of oppression that Black women face. The experiences that people with intersecting identities now face are the reason why the term has become more mainstream. Moya Bailey coined a newer term, misogynoir, to describe "the specific hatred, dislike, distrust, and prejudice directed toward Black women." Anti-racism education and efforts must explore misogynoir, how it manifests, and how it can be mitigated.

Misogynoir is rampant in ways that may not even be realized. The hashtag #SayHerName was created in 2014 to highlight misogynoir and how stories of Black women and girls often go overlooked, unnoticed, and untold. These experiences range from police violence to sexual assault, and often go unreported. Two very apparent examples of misogynoir in the public sphere can be found in the stories of musician R. Kelly's victims and, most recently, the events that transpired with rapper Megan Thee Stallion.

---

169 Crenshaw, Kimberlé. 1991. "Mapping the Margins: Intersectionality, Identity Politics, and Violence against Women of Color." *Stanford Law Review* 43, no. 6 (July): 1241–1299.

protecting my peace

Throughout R. Kelly's thirty-year career, a number of women and girls, mostly Black and underage, have made claims that R. Kelly has sexually abused them. Despite the growing number of accusations, it wasn't until recently, when the 2019 documentary *Surviving R. Kelly* came out, that these stories were given credence. Black women and girls who share experiences of abuse, trauma, and assault are largely shunned, criticized, and ignored. These experiences are questioned, scrutinized, and dissected more than any other group.[170]

According to the National Black Women's Justice Institute, Black women and girls have been stereotyped as promiscuous and hypersexual for centuries, and that stereotype continues today. The "Strong Black Woman" stereotype means that we are less likely to be seen as victims. Our mental health and well-being are minimized or disregarded. Our trauma remains unacknowledged and unaddressed. And the very institutions and organizations in charge of providing us with that protection—such as schools, hospitals, and mental health facilities—leave us unprotected.

Sexual trauma is frequently associated with PTSD, depression, substance misuse, suicide ideation and attempts, and other adverse health effects. For Black women, the added effects of sexism and racism can heighten depressive and PTSD symptoms. When trauma is unaddressed, it leaves us more at risk of interaction with law enforcement and the legal system because, often, the way we express our trauma does not conform to traditional clinical symptoms. As a result, we are criminalized instead of receiving the treatment and care we need and deserve.

Additionally, the strategies that Black women and girls take to survive are often criminalized, creating an abuse-to-incarceration pipeline that

170   Asare, Janice G. 2020. "Misogynoir: The Unique Discrimination That Black Women Face." *Forbes*, September 22, 2020. www.forbes.com/sites/janicegassam/2020/09/22/misogynoir-the-unique-discrimination-that-black-women-face/?sh=3b673fa956ef.

overwhelmingly targets Black women and girls.[171] And this snowball effect of trauma begins with the adultification of Black girls by a society that views them as older, more mature, and less deserving of protection. According to the landmark Georgetown University study "Girlhood Interrupted: The Erasure of Black Girls' Childhood," scholars found substantial evidence of adultification of Black girls. The study reveals how society often prematurely assigns adult characteristics to young Black girls, consequently erasing their childhood. Noting that our society "regularly responds to Black girls as if they are fully developed adults," Dr. Monique W. Morris has observed, "The assignment of more adult-like characteristics to the expressions of young Black girls is a form of age compression. Along this truncated age continuum, Black girls are likened more to adults than to children, and are treated as if they are willfully engaging in behaviors typically expected of Black women. This compression [has] stripped Black girls of their childhood freedoms [and] rendered Black girlhood interchangeable with Black womanhood."[172]

These perceptions, often resulting in Black girls being viewed as older than they are, demonstrate that stereotypes of them as "loud" carry adult-like connotations and cause them to be seen as a threat. In a recent study focused on teacher-student interactions by Professor Edward W. Morris, one teacher's comment stood out: "[Black girls] think they are adults too, and they try to act like they should have control sometimes." This comment was made in the context of classroom management, showing how Black girls' assertiveness can be misconstrued as inappropriate maturity.[173] Such comments demonstrate that stereotypes of Black girls, interpreted as "loud," are imbued with adult-like aspirations and perceived, in turn, as a threat. The same study recorded teachers' descriptions of Black girls as

171 "Black Women, Sexual Assault, and Criminalization." 2020. National Black Women's Justice Institute. www.nbwji.org/post/black-women-sexual-assault-criminalization.

172 Morris, Monique W. 2016. *Pushout: The Criminalization of Black Girls in Schools.* New York: New Press.

173 Morris, Edward W. 2007. " 'Ladies' or 'Loudies'?: Perceptions and Experiences of Black Girls in Classrooms." *Youth & Society* 38, no. 4 (June): 490–515.

exhibiting "very 'mature' behavior that is socially (but not academically) sophisticated and 'controlling at a young age.' " This interpretation of Black girls' outspokenness may be associated with the stereotype of Black women as aggressive and dominating.[174][175]

Another harmful aspect of adultification for Black girls lies in the culturally embedded stereotypes about Black girls' sexualization.[176] The commonly held stereotype of Black girls as hypersexualized is defined by "society's attribution of sex as part of the 'natural' role of Black women and girls."[177] Noting the long history of perceiving Black women as hypersexualized, Monique W. Morris has observed that adultification results in applying these stereotypes to Black girls:

> Caricatures of Black femininity are often deposited into distinct chambers of our public consciousness, narrowly defining Black female identity and movement according to the stereotypes described by Pauli Murray as "female dominance" on the one hand and loose morals on the other hand, both growing out of the roles forced upon them during the slavery experience and its aftermath. As such, in the public's collective consciousness, latent ideas about Black females as hypersexual, conniving, loud, and sassy predominate. However, age compression renders Black girls just as vulnerable to these aspersive representations.[178]

The images and historical stereotypes of Black women aren't just relics of the past. They continue to have real-life consequences for Black girls today. According to

174 Morris, Monique, 2016.

175 Nanda, Jyoti. 2012. "Blind Discretion: Girls of Color & Delinquency in the Juvenile Justice System." *59 UCLA L. rev. 1502, 1521,* (August).

176 Morris, Monique, 2016.

177 Dagbovie-Mullins, Sika A. 2013. "Pigtails, Ponytails, and Getting Tail: The Infantilization and Hyper-Sexualization of African American Females in Popular Culture." *The Journal of Popular Culture* 46 (August): 745–771.

178 Morris, Monique. 2016.

Blake and colleagues, "these stereotypes underlie the implicit bias that shapes many adult views of Black females [as] ...sexually promiscuous, hedonistic, and in need of socialization."[179]

In essence, "the adultification stereotype results in some [Black] children not being afforded the opportunity" to make mistakes and to learn, grow, and benefit from correction for youthful missteps to the same degree as white children. The Georgetown University study shows that Black girls experience this stereotype directly.[180]

We know that these stereotypes have been used to silence our strong forces and create resistance to our embracing the full power of the divine feminine that resides inside all of us as women of the African diaspora. So how do we harness that power while disavowing and divesting from these harmful, toxic, and false representations? It starts with amplifying our voices, embracing our individuality, and consciously rejecting these harmful stereotypes. For me, this mindset shift meant decolonizing and recalibrating my mind. It involved surrounding myself with positive representations of Black womanhood, seeking out inspiring stories and powerful figures from our history, and reminding myself daily that we are the descendants of humanity's birthplace.

To protect our peace, it is very necessary to begin the process of decolonizing our minds: replacing old thoughts and beliefs with traditional Afrocentric ideals rooted in our authentically native ancestry. In thinking about my own identity as a Black woman, I'd often fallen victim to many of the stereotypes and carried

179 Blake, Jamilia J., Bettie R. Butler, and Danielle Smith. 2015. "Challenging Middle-Class Notions of Femininity: The Cause of Black Females' Disproportionate Suspension Rates." In *Closing the School Discipline Gap: Equitable Remedies for Excessive Exclusion*, edited by Daniel J. Losen. New York: Teachers College Press.

180 Epstein, Rebecca, Jamilia J. Blake, and Thalia Gonzalez. 2017. "Girlhood Interrupted: The Erasure of Black Girls' Childhood." The Center on Gender Justice & Opportunity at Georgetown Law. genderjusticeandopportunity.georgetown.edu/wp-content/uploads/2020/06/girlhood-interrupted.pdf.

those narratives with me both mentally and physically. It affects how we show up, our own ideals about womanhood, our mental and emotional well-being, and even our very identity.

At times, we feel like ships adrift in the sea. We know how we feel inside, but we don't feel that our actions match our intent as we move. Are we being too loud, too quiet, too outspoken, or not assertive enough? Are we dressed appropriately? Do we meet the expectations of our community? What about our families? And even more intimidating, how do we appear to the world? All of the confusion about what we represent in our physical and symbolic essence can be absolutely exhausting. And without anywhere to seek answers to those questions, we often internalize this disconnect, thinking there is something inherently wrong with us when what has actually happened is a trauma response to a society that has created a rendition that is entirely not of our making.

The process of deconstructing these ideas began in my Black community in Fort Lauderdale, where I was nurtured and encouraged about my identity and greatness. I was told that not only was I worthy, I was more than worthy. And although I didn't see myself represented in society at large, everyone close to me reflected positive energy centered on my perfect existence. It wasn't until I ventured out of those safe spaces into environments that didn't look like me that I started to doubt the perfection of my identity. I had always been charged with the responsibility of loving not only myself, but everyone else around me who looked like me. I was part of a resilient community that, despite material limitations, showered me with love, wisdom, and a strong sense of belonging.

Going into predominantly white spaces, the clarion call was the opposite. On the first day of orientation, I was told to look both left and right, and that neither student would be there at graduation. In my classes, I was anonymous—one of thousands. The safest course of action was to blend in with everyone around me. The only problem with that philosophy was that it was impossible. And even if it were possible, I knew deep inside that I would never want that to happen.

To counter these feelings of displacement and loss, Simphiwe Sesanti, a professor at the University of the Western Cape (UWC)'s Faculty of Education, calls for "Decolonized and Afrocentric Education: For Centering African Women in Remembering, Re-Membering, and the African Renaissance." Decolonization was a widespread effort, spanning both the African continent and its diaspora. It was a fight against the influences of European slavery and colonialism. This movement symbolized an African Renaissance—a rebirth and reclamation of our culture. Colonialism and colonization dismembered Africans through land dispossession and forcible relocation into slavery. Both the physical and cultural dismemberment were entrenched and sustained through Eurocentric education, which sought to displace Africans' cultural memory by replacing it with European cultural memory. Decolonization struggles were an expression of an African Renaissance because they sought to "regain" and "restore" not only physical but also cultural freedom.[181]

The revolutionary Pan-Africanist scholar, academic, and activist, W. E. B. Du Bois, declared in his book *The Souls of Black Folk*, first published in 1903, that "THE PROBLEM of the twentieth century is the problem of the color line—the relation of the darker to lighter races of men in Asia and Africa, in America and the islands of the sea."[182]

In his book *Dark Water: Voices From Within The Veil*, published seventeen years later, Du Bois pointed out that the "uplift of women is, next to the problem of the color line and the peace movement, our greatest modern

181 Sesanti, Simphiwe. 2019. "Decolonized and Afrocentric Education: For Centering African Women in Remembering, Re-Membering, and the African Renaissance." *Journal of Black Studies* 50 (5): 431–449.

182 Du Bois, W. E. B. 1989. *The Souls of Black Folk*. New York: Bantam Classic Books.

cause." Du Bois further pointed out that when "two of these movements—woman and color—combine in one, the combination has deep meaning."

Du Bois's logic was informed by recognition, not only that the oppression and exploitation of African Americans was unnatural and wrong, but also that the struggle for the dignity of Black women in the United States was about the reclamation of an African culture that slavery dealt a blow to. His studies on ancient African history had taught him that in Africa "none is more tenderly loved than the Negro mother." Du Bois had learned that:

- "Everywhere in Africa [...] no greater affront can be offered a Negro than insulting his mother." He discovered that the Krus, the Fantis, and the Mandingo could withstand an enemy's blows, but would not put up with abuse directed toward their mothers.

- Among the Dyoor, Du Bois learned that "[a] bond between mother and child which lasts for life is the measure of affection shown."

- Among the Zulu-speaking Africans and the Waganda, Du Bois found that "the mother is the most influential counselor at the court of ferocious sovereigns, like Chaka or Mtesa; sometimes sisters take her place."

In these African cultures, Du Bois learned that women were held in high esteem. Evidence for this could be seen in the many queens, the respect given to medicine women, and the participation of women in public meetings in many African societies.

On the basis of his studies on Africa, Du Bois concluded that this picture appeared as if "the great Black race, in passing up the steps of human culture, gave the world not only the Iron Age, the cultivation of the soil, and the domestication of animals, but also, in peculiar emphasis, the mother-idea."[183]

---

183   Du Bois, W. E. B. 1999. *Dark Water: Voices From Within The Veil.* New York: Dover Publications.

The "mother-idea" refers to all that is mentioned above—the centering, the veneration, and the love for womanhood. The "mother-idea" refers to the "sacredness and infallibility of mothers," which finds expression in an Igbo woman song: "Woman is principal, is principal, is principal."[184] The African "mother-idea" also finds expression in the Ohaffia proverb, "Father's penis scatters, mother's womb gathers," a saying that is both literal and metaphorical.[185] The African "mother-idea" was disrupted (among some)—but not destroyed—in the African American community because "the westward slave trade and American slavery struck like doom." Against the "doom" of American slavery, the "mother-idea" remained a constant in the Black community and characterized the uniquely esteemed and elevated role of womanhood across the African diaspora.

Many African Americans held on tenaciously to their ancestral cultural beliefs that defined their humanity. A conversation between Maya Angelou, a Pan-Africanist and world-renowned poetess, and Nana Nketsia, the University of Ghana's first vice chancellor, reveals as much. Nana Nketsia addressed Angelou:

> You are a mother and we love our mothers [...] Africa is herself a mother. The mother of mankind. We Africans take motherhood as the most sacred condition human beings can achieve. Camara Laye, our brother, has said, "The Mother is there to protect you. She is buried in Africa, and Africa is buried in her. That is why she is supreme."

Angelou reciprocated, affirming the enduring cultural bonds between Africans on the continent and in the Diaspora, bonds that defied the ravages of slavery.

184 Amadiume, Ifi. 1989. "Introduction: Cheikh Anta Diop's theory of matriarchal values as the basis for African cultural unity." In *The Cultural Unity of Black Africa: The Domains of Matriarchy & of Patriarchy in Classical Antiquity* London: Karnak House.

185 Kamalu, Chukwunyere. 1990. *Foundations of African Thought: A Worldview Grounded in the African Heritage of Religion, Philosophy, Science and Art.* London: Karnak House.

protecting my peace

Nana, I appreciate hearing that Africans cherish their mothers. It confirms my belief that in America we have retained more Africanisms than we know. For also, among Black Americans, motherhood is sacred. We have strong mothers, and we love them dearly.[186]

Echoing Du Bois's stance against sexism, Professor Sesanti emphasizes that the fight is not a one-time event, but a continual effort. He proposes this can be achieved through a decolonized, Afrocentric education. An Afrocentric "education system should be such that the children are taught that the natural line of descent is through the mother." This can be demonstrated beyond doubt once it is understood that all human beings are conceived by women. Through Afrocentric education, children should be made aware that the traits of both sexes exist within each human being: within every man there is a woman, and within every woman there is a man. Therefore, any man who hates women is a man who hates an aspect of himself that he cannot come to terms with. His hatred for women is therefore an externalization of this self-hatred.[187]

Sitting in the Women in Africa class my junior year helped me learn, just as my ancestors, W.E.B. DuBois and Maya Angelou, had learned before me. I was the descendant of a lineage of Black women in Africa who were not characterized by any of the harmful and toxic stereotypes, archetypes, and descriptions that had done nothing to empower me, but had been deliberately deployed by those in the majority to disarm and erode my self-confidence, leading to doubt in myself and my identity while eroding my mental health and emotional well-being, making me question everything around me, including my very existence. Instead, I recaptured the feeling of joy and belonging I felt inside when my African American studies teacher smiled at me and called me "Amina" when I was in the eleventh grade.

186 Angelou, Maya. 2008. *All God's Children Need Traveling Shoes*. New York: Virago Press.
187 Kamalu, Chukwunyere, *Foundations of African Thought: A Worldview Grounded in the African Heritage of Religion, Philosophy, Science and Art.*

journaling questions

1. How do you connect with or perceive the concept of the African Sacred Feminine, and what significance does it hold for you?

2. What steps can you take to deepen your understanding and connection to the African Sacred Feminine, given its potential transformative power?

3. Can you identify specific stereotypes of Black women that have impacted you personally, either by being imposed upon you or through internalized beliefs?

4. What strategies or practices have you found effective in challenging and countering harmful stereotypes about Black women, both externally and within yourself?

5. In what ways have societal perceptions of Black women influenced your interactions, opportunities, or self-perception?

6. How do you think these societal perceptions and stereotypes manifest in tangible consequences for Black women in various spheres like the workplace, relationships, and personal well-being?

7. What does the concept of "decolonizing the mind" mean to you, especially as a Black woman navigating a world filled with colonized narratives?

8. Can you identify moments or experiences in your life that have contributed to your journey of decolonizing your mind and reclaiming your authentic self?

9. How can you actively engage in deconstructing stereotypes, not just for yourself, but to help shift societal narratives about Black women at large?

10. How does being part of a supportive community of Black women facilitate the process of decolonizing the mind and challenging stereotypes?

affirmations

1. I am deeply rooted in the African Sacred Feminine, channeling its power, wisdom, and nurturing spirit.

2. The strength of countless generations of powerful Black women flows within me, guiding and sustaining me.

3. I rise above stereotypes, knowing that my worth and identity are not defined by society's narrow perceptions.

4. I am authentically me, embracing my unique journey and experiences, undeterred by external judgments.

5. Every day, I reclaim my narrative, actively decolonizing my mind and breaking free from limiting beliefs.

6. I challenge and change societal perceptions, recognizing that my voice and presence matter.

7. I am on a continuous path of healing and growth, shedding the weight of imposed stereotypes and embracing my true self.

8. I draw strength from my ancestors, standing tall on their shoulders, and honoring their legacy through my actions.

9. I am part of a vibrant community of Black women, and together we uplift, support, and empower one another.

10. I am a beautiful blend of history, culture, resilience, and wisdom, and I wear each facet with pride.

the drums of Africa still beat in my heart.

chapter 10

reflecting on precolonial societies and their relevance today

"For I am my mother's daughter,
and the drums of Africa still beat in my heart."

—Mary McLeod Bethune

Protecting our peace involves recapturing the true essence of who we are at our ancestral core, both as Black women and, as Du Bois noted, as the mothers of civilization. It was in my Women in Africa class that I learned how sacred the role of African women was in antiquity. This was the history that was taken and hidden. It is our strength and universal knowledge that allow us to tap into the higher frequency that vibrates inside us and embodies who we truly are at our core. That empty space that I felt was filled with the knowledge that I came from a legacy of culture where matrilineal and matriarchal systems provided women with power, autonomy, and a central role in society.

However, it's important to understand the challenges that Afrocentric education is up against. The underlying principles of patriarchy, which have dictated societal norms for centuries, are separation and control. During colonization, for instance, the fundamental decisions affecting the lives of colonized people were made and implemented by colonial rulers in pursuit of interests that were often defined in a distant metropolis. This brings us to an important term, "the feminization of poverty," a phrase conceptualized by Diana Pearce in 1978. She observed this trend in her studies of women in America, but it's a pattern that extends beyond national borders.[188] Although poverty is a national and international social impediment, women tend to be most vulnerable. She observed that two-thirds of the poor were women over the age of sixteen, and an increasingly large number were from economically disadvantaged groups. The discourse on "the feminization of poverty" holds that, as a result of the recession and reduced public spending by governments, women are increasingly represented among the world's poor.[189] Yet, it is crucial to remember that in precolonial times, women were economic powerhouses in Africa.

188   Pearce, Diana. 1978. "The Feminization of Poverty: Women, Work, and Welfare." *Urban and Social Change Review* 11 (1): 28–36.

189   Veeran, Vasintha. 2000. "Feminization of Poverty." *International Conference of the International Association of the Schools of Social Work* 29 (July).

Ancient Africans held a deep-seated respect for women. This respect was reflected in their social structures, family roles, and religious practices. The respect that ancient Africans had for women is well documented. As Dr. Charles S. Finch III, an Egyptian scholar, illustrates in his book *Echoes of the Old Darkland*, early men didn't even realize the link between sex and birth; such was the degree of reverence and mystique surrounding women. Therefore, it was believed that new life was created by the woman alone. It was perceived that all life in nature emerged from women alone. When the first concept of God was developed, the female served as the model of the Supreme Being.[190]

It is not known exactly when the role of the male in procreation was discovered, but this discovery did not enhance the status of men. Their status only became elevated when the necessity of men became clear in war and conquest. In ancient Egypt and Kush, the importance of the mother was seen in the fact that the children took their surname from the mother. The mother controlled both the household and the fields. In Kush, the Queen Mother had the right to choose the next Pharaoh.

Prior to the Islamic conquest of sub-Saharan Africa in the twelfth and thirteenth centuries, the system of succession to the throne was matrilineal. Matrilineality refers not only to tracing one's lineage through maternal ancestry; it can also refer to a civil system in which one inherits property through the female line. In *Pre-Colonial Black Africa*, Senegalese historian and anthropologist Cheikh Anta Diop explains that, in the African custom of matrilineal succession, very strict rules were observed. The heir to the throne was not the king's son, but the son of the King's first-born sister (the king's nephew). It was said: "You can never be sure who the father of the child is, but of the mother you can always be sure."[191]

190 Finch, Charles. 1991. *Echoes of the Old Darkland: Themes from the African Eden.* Decatur: Khenti, Incorporated.

191 Diop, Cheikh A. 1987. *Precolonial Black Africa: A Comparative Study of the Political and Social Systems of Europe and Black Africa, from Antiquity to the Formation of Modern States.* Translated by Harold Salemson. Brooklyn: Lawrence Hill Books.

African societies adopted this view to ensure that power and titles of leadership were conferred through the mother's lines. This matriarchal foundation of African society meant that respect for women was woven into the very fabric of society. African social organization was fundamentally built around the matriclan, wherein one's identity, inheritance, wealth, and politics are all determined. All matriclan founders were female, but men traditionally held leadership positions within the society. These inherited roles, however, are passed down matrilineally, meaning through a man's mothers and sisters (and their children). Women remained indispensable to the reproduction of communities in matrilineal societies, for their bloodlines defined the transmission of both office and wealth.

Women were the major food producers, and thus not only had ready access to land but also had authority over how the land was to be used and cultivated. The value of women's productive labor in producing and processing food established and maintained their rights in the domestic and other spheres. Lobola, a customary Southern African dowry practice, gave women a certain amount of economic independence and clout. In the past, African women retained a measure of control over their lobola, which economically empowered them.

Foreign invasions, particularly Islam and later European colonialism, significantly exacerbated and hastened the erosion of women's status. It's a common misconception, held by both Africans and non-Africans, that the current status of women in Africa mirrors their status in 'traditional African societies.' This, however, isn't accurate.

What is correct is that missionary activities and the desire of European missionaries to recreate African families into monogamous and nuclear units were possibly the biggest contributors to the sidelining of women's earning power and their ability to claim the proceeds of their labor. Even the development of legal systems under colonialism guaranteed that women were at a disadvantage, as "customary" laws were often established based on male testimony alone. This gave men, especially elite men, advantages over women in issues of marriage and divorce.

The colonial production system, which excluded women from the cash economy, was imported by missionaries, and the colonial wage economy was essentially a male one. A significant contributing factor to the persistent gender inequality in Africa was the introduction of a gender-biased educational system by missionaries. During colonial times, the introduction of cash crops and women's subsequent exclusion from the global marketplace greatly diminished women's power and economic autonomy. Even further, men and international commerce benefited because they were able to rely to some extent on women's unremunerated labor.

In precolonial Africa, women's significant role in agricultural production meant their labor was necessary; it was the labor that yielded surplus.[192] It was women who developed the practice of purposeful cultivation and were responsible for food production. There is also strong linguistic and archaeological evidence to point to women's strong social and political authority across Africa.

Indications are that avenues for female political representation were only closed off during the colonial period. Patriarchal alliances struck between various colonial administrations and African chiefs and elders resulted in the systematization and codification of patriarchy across African societies. Women's precolonial political activity was generally disregarded by the colonial authorities, who turned exclusively to men when they established local political offices. In many parts of Africa, women were members of associations run by and for women, which gave women the final say in disputes over markets or agriculture. The colonial agents, nearly always men, ignored that reality.

---

192 Saidi, Christine. 2010. *Women's Authority and Society in Early East-Central Africa.* New York: University of Rochester Press.

In the past, African societies had a dual-sex political system that allowed for substantial female representation and involvement in governance. Cheikh Anta Diop explains bicameralism, a type of governance our ancestors used to rule their people. Before Africa came under the dominance of any foreign powers, women had a position of influence in society. A key aspect of precolonial African political structure was bicameralism, wherein women had their own separate assembly distinct from the men's assembly. Despite their separate natures, these assemblies shared influence and power, reflecting the valued role of women in public affairs. This assembly sat separately from the man's assembly, but the two shared influence and power. The resistance against foreign invasion and occupation of West African nations such as Dahomey (Benin) and the Yorubas in Nigeria is said to be a result of the women's assembly meeting at night. African bicameralism allowed the blossoming of both males and females and allowed the full use of both the feminine and masculine minds.[193]

Bicameralism is an ancient example of African democracy that made full use of the human resources of society in a manner that supported and encouraged everyone. In modern times, prominent figures like Winnie Mandela have continued the call for women's empowerment. Mandela contended that women should rise up to challenge their marginalization in male-dominated society by declaring "nothing about us without us" and encouraging them to take active roles in all social and political structures.[194]

Historian Ivor Wilks refers to the sixteenth century in African history as the "era of great ancestresses," a time characterized by egalitarian social structures. According to C. Magbaily Fyle, Professor in the African American Studies and African Studies departments at the Ohio State University, although men dominated politics in Africa in the precolonial period, there were quite a few women who played an active role in politics and government. Africa, with its

---

193 Diop, 1987.

194 Okrah, Kwadwo A. 2017. "The dynamics of gender roles and cultural determinants of African women's desire to participate in modern politics." *Scholar Works*, 1–15.

diverse cultures and traditions, has experienced variations in the roles and status of women. While women were generally not subservient to men, their exercise of power and authority was not uniform across the continent.

- For instance, among the Sotho of South Africa, daughters of sub-rulers were heads of women's regiments, showing the direct involvement of women in governance and military affairs. Another example is found during the reign of Sigidi ka Senzangakhona, also known as Shaka. His aunt Mkabayi and Queen Mother Nandi were given substantial authority, placed in charge of military kraals, and empowered to govern while the Emperor was on campaign.

- In Niger and Chad, women led migrations, formed cities, and conquered kingdoms, such as Queen Amina of Katsina (Songhai people).

- In Yoruba political culture, there was the Iyalode, who was a member of the Alafin's council. This was the judiciary body in Yoruba.

- The Iyalode was a female representative who was responsible for women's issues and their spokeswoman at the Alafin's meetings.

- In Sierra Leone, among the Mende and Sherbro people, by the nineteenth century, women could be heads of towns and sub-regions.[195]

The African cultural concepts of "rights in persons" (the value of individual human capabilities) and "wealth in people" (the importance of human resources) placed a significant value on women's labor and procreation. Colonial powers understood this, and thus the most important project of colonialism was to destroy the African family structure, as this is the most important economic and political institution.

Ultimately, the patriarchal assumptions of European colonial administrators and missionaries shaped colonial economic structures and gender-biased education

---

195 Fyle, C. M. 1999. *Introduction to the History of African Civilization*. Lanham: University Press Of America.

systems. These changes, in turn, enabled African chiefs and male elders to orchestrate a social coup. Therefore, it's important to reassess our understanding of African women's status as "traditional." This label often misrepresents historical and cultural realities and can prevent us from fully acknowledging and addressing the challenges they face today. In many cases, colonizers manipulated what we now recognize as our customary law to impose patriarchal norms. They often co-opted, distorted, or reinvented local traditions to justify and entrench the subordination of women, a legacy that continues to impact the status of women in society.[196]

According to Professor Emerita and former chair of the Women's Spirituality Program at the California Institute of Integral Studies, Arisika Razak, many early African cultures did not separate the sacred and secular dimensions of life, but created images that depicted Black women as sacred embodiments of social, spiritual, and cultural power. While individuals of diverse sexual orientations and diverse genders exist in Africa as they do everywhere else in the world, the cultural and artistic celebration of the African Sacred Feminine was a part of many precolonial African societies.

In their ancestral African cultures, both men and women revered female deities and elemental powers, and today, people of all genders still do so in a few instances from Nigeria. Although many spiritually-based North, Central, and West African cultures were patriarchal, they still acknowledged the existence of male and female deities and affirmed the spiritual power, political authority, and social leadership of women.[197]

Razak asserts that, in spite of imposed sexist gender norms, African American culture affirms Black women's leadership. Take, for example, the pivotal roles

---

196   Shandu, Mthiya. 2018. "A Stolen Legacy: The Matrilineality of Pre-Colonial African Society." Medium. medium.com/@MthiyaneShandu/a-stolen-legacy-the-matrilineality-of-pre-colonial-african-society-5307b8db3e5a.

197   Razak, Arisika. "Sacred Women of Africa and the African Diaspora: A Womanist Vision of Black Women's Bodies and the African Sacred Feminine." *International Journal of Transpersonal Studies* 35 (2016): 14.

played by women in the Civil Rights Movement and other liberation struggles that served the interests of the entire population, regardless of gender. In addition, historical images of the African Sacred Feminine offer a healing template for the wounds of racial misogyny that African American women still experience with regard to their bodies, their sexualities, and their social and spiritual roles. [198] Furthermore, the activism, leadership, and spiritual power of iconic African American women such as Harriet Tubman, Sojourner Truth, and Ida B. Wells,[199] who all embody the womanist ideals of Black feminism professed by Alice Walker, are rooted in West African cultural concepts that viewed spiritual power, economic prowess, physical strength, and political authority as characteristics shared by all genders and therefore characteristic of both the masculine and feminine realms.[200]

African Americans in the United States celebrate many new spiritual traditions. Some of these traditions emanate from the Black church, while others draw from African-derived traditions. These African roots can be traced back to various cultures, including Yoruba, Fon, Igbo, Dahomean, and Khemetic sources. They provided African Americans of both sexes with potential sites of resistance to racist oppression[201] and reflected West African concepts of women's power. Among the Ibo and Yoruba, women held power as individuals[202] and as members of female collectives, which were part of dual-gendered systems of social, spiritual, and political power.[203] These collectives enabled women to challenge,

198 Walker, Alice. 1983. *In Search of Our Mothers' Gardens: Womanist Prose.* San Diego: Harcourt Brace Jovanovich.

199 Davis, Angela. 1983. *Women, race, & class.* Vancouver: Vintage Books.

200 Badejo, Diedre. 1996. *Osun Seegesi: The Elegant Deity of Wealth, Power, and Femininity.* Trenton: Africa World Press.

201 Goboldte, Catherine. 2002. "Laying on hands: Women in Imani faith temple." In *My Soul is a Witness: African-American Women's Spirituality,* edited by Gloria Wade-Gayles, 241–252. Boston: Beacon Press.

202 Amadiume, Ifi. 1987. *Male daughters, female husbands: gender and sex in an African society.* London: Zed Books.

203 Badejo, 1996.

critique, punish, and make war against individual men, as well as masculine collectives and colonial bureaucracies.[204]

My studies, particularly my Women in Africa class, which I proudly passed with an A, greatly influenced not only my academic understanding, but also my personal outlook. I began to see myself and the legacy of Black women through a different lens. This newfound knowledge also reframed the way I looked at other Black women and my legacy of greatness. I knew that it was rooted in matriarchy, or even more accurately, in bicameralism, where women participated in the running of public affairs within the framework of a women's assembly. Our lineage was passed down through matrilineal lines, with women's power, political authority, and social leadership central to the fabric of the collective good of the community. Again, like the understanding of our beauty, the energy that we transmit is one of the divine feminine, and our legacy is one of immense power that has no home within the false and harmful stereotypes of the Strong Black Woman, the Sapphire, or the Jezebel. By harnessing this truth, I started to embrace my power as innate and ordained by my ancestors, rather than a mark of aggression or lack of self-control.

Moreover, I came to understand that decolonizing my mind would be a lifelong journey. It entails recalling and relearning my true story, a narrative that my ancestors had to endure during the processes of colonization, enslavement, and displacement. By embracing the truth about how wonderful we are in every way and how worthy we are to be both admired and revered in a central role of respect, we honor what our ancestors wanted for us. They made the ultimate sacrifice to ensure our minds remained free, regardless of the physical bondage our ancestors suffered over generations. To honor that sacrifice, it's important that I uphold a legacy of greatness, intelligence, and excellence. Embracing Black excellence means more than subscribing to notions of "working twice

204 Van Allen, J. 1972. "Sitting on a man: Colonialism and the lost political institutions of Igbo women." *Canadian Journal of African Studies* 6 (2): 165–181.

as hard," chronic burnout, "grinding," stress, and "hustle culture." Instead, it's about choosing to embody the woman I was destined to be, a destiny etched in the blood that runs through my veins. My divinity affords me autonomy and the right to choose how I present myself and interact with the world. I create life not just with my womb but with my thoughts, my words, and my actions. That is true divine energy.

True freedom comes from understanding our past, not only on the American continent but across the African diaspora and back to antiquity in precolonial Africa. Understanding our truth creates a barrier against being oppressed, subjugated, or mentally enslaved by harmful constructs. Such accounts often inflict damage on our mental health and emotional well-being, leaving us with a persistent feeling that something is missing. The missing piece is our authentic self-identity. We are embodiments of divine femininity, a philosophy of reverence for the goddesses of the original civilizations, civilizations that were the cradle of all humankind. Fully understanding and internalizing this truth is crucial for maintaining our peace, as it equips us with the power to guard against discord. Fully understanding and embracing this truth is vital for fostering inner peace, a state I consider crucial for my well-being. When I talk about protecting my peace, it means maintaining self-assuredness in my identity, values, and worth. It means not allowing external opinions to shake my self-perception, because I am confident in who I am. I am the beginning and the end because I have always been. Our legacy predates any other, and it will persist indefinitely. We are both the beginning and the end—Alpha and Omega. Our existence and influence have always been there, and they will continue to shape the world.

Affirming ourselves and staying true to our identity is an ongoing process that requires constant reflection and action. It takes time to divest from images that dictate our appearance according to the ideals of beauty ingrained in whiteness. Focusing on our own beauty both inside and out is not only the way for us to embrace our real identities, but it's also a way to pay homage to all of the women from our ancestral lineage who paved the way forward for us to exist today.

We are not, and have never been, the archetypes and stereotypes that have misrepresented our true identity and undermined our self-perception.

I intentionally surround myself with images—whether they are in the artwork on my office walls, my clothing, or my jewelry—that reflect our inherent beauty and femininity. I want to reflect who my ancestral mothers wanted me to be and the amazing physical energy that radiates from within me, provided by them. By doing so, I honor who I am and who I will always be. I also model what I want for the women around me as a collective. Our beauty, energy, and femininity are collective forces that span time and space. That energy is unstoppable, if we believe in its power instead of the harmful and toxic falsehoods we have been spoon-fed that erode our mental health and emotional well-being by causing us anxiety and chipping away at our confidence and self-esteem. What we feed our minds matters. Filling our minds with positivity requires us to continually affirm and appreciate our innate beauty, perfection, and wonderful complexity. It means ignoring anything that doesn't feed our truth. It means disavowing any story that doesn't speak to who we really are.

Therefore, it is our responsibility to uphold our truth and reclaim our identity. We can't rely on a society to provide something they never wanted us to be. Rather, they have actively worked to deprive us of our true nature and the power it holds, but that true power and energy are vibrating at such a high frequency that they can never be denied. We witness the impact of this inherent power around us every day. This visible proof starkly contrasts the harmful stereotypes imposed upon us, ideas that are in conflict with our reality and disturb our well-deserved peace. We can never find true peace by accepting an identity that does not align with our authentic selves. The truth is, we are not defined by any of the narratives ascribed to us by society. We are not and have never been "Angry Black Women," "Strong Black Women," "Jezebels," "Sapphires," or "Mammies." We don't ascribe to anything that forces us to compromise our divine femininity. We are, and always have been, queens in our own right. Our lineage starts and will last forever at the beginning of time.

journaling questions

1. How does the concept of feminine divinity across the African diaspora resonate with your personal understanding and embodiment of Black womanhood?

2. In what ways have harmful stereotypes and archetypes about Black womanhood influenced your personal perception of your own femininity, and how can you work toward decolonizing these perceptions?

3. How can the practice of daily decolonization serve as a form of self-care and empowerment for you as a Black woman?

4. In what ways does the understanding and honoring of feminine divinity help challenge and counteract the oppressive narratives that have been crafted about Black womanhood?

5. How do you feel the portrayal of Black women in media and society impacts your personal identity and self-perception?

6. How can connecting with the concept of feminine divinity across the African diaspora help foster a sense of unity and collective identity among Black women?

7. How have you seen or experienced the harmful effects of negative stereotypes about Black womanhood in your own life, and what strategies have you employed to overcome or counteract them?

8. What tangible actions can you take to further decolonize your mind and remove any internalized negative perceptions about Black womanhood?

9. How do you incorporate the practice of decolonization into your daily routine, and how has this practice influenced your perspective on self-care as a Black woman?

10. How can a commitment to a long-term practice of decolonization and a deeper understanding of feminine divinity contribute to a holistic and healthy perspective of your identity as a Black woman?

affirmations

1. I embrace and honor the divine femininity within me as a Black woman, knowing that it is a powerful force that connects me to my ancestral roots.

2. I am proud of my unique beauty as a Black woman, celebrating the richness of my melanin and the diverse features that make me who I am.

3. I am deserving of love, respect, and acceptance just as I am, understanding that my worth is not defined by society's narrow standards of beauty.

4. My voice as a Black woman is valuable and important, and I have the right to express myself authentically and be heard.

5. I am resilient and strong, embodying the spirit of my ancestors, who fought against adversity and paved the way for me to thrive.

6. I embrace my heritage and cultural identity, recognizing the wisdom and traditions passed down through generations of Black women.

7. I honor my emotions and intuition, knowing that they are powerful guides that connect me to my inner wisdom and strength.

8. I am capable of achieving my goals and dreams, defying stereotypes and limitations that may seek to hold me back.

9. I celebrate the sisterhood of Black women, knowing that we are a source of support, inspiration, and empowerment for one another.

10. I love and accept myself unconditionally, embracing all aspects of my being as a Black woman and recognizing the beauty and power that reside within me.

protect your peace!

A Conclusion

The journey of the African American woman, as explored in *Protecting My Peace*, is a profound tapestry of endurance, resilience, and a rootedness in rich cultural heritage. This book is a tribute to every Black woman navigating the intricate terrains of identity, past pains, and societal demands; it casts light on the path to inner tranquility, merging lessons from the past with contemporary insights and resources.

The obstacles Black women encounter span both historical burdens like chattel slavery and entrenched discrimination, as well as present-day societal pressures, such as media stereotyping and workplace inequities, that foster biases. However, this book emphasized the crucial process of recognizing, understanding, and healing from these challenges. By valuing Black history and culture, addressing both emotional wounds and systemic barriers, emphasizing holistic well-being, and advocating for a fairer society, a clear route to individual peace and collective advancement emerges.

Throughout the book, I accentuated the value of a supportive community. I underscored the importance of acknowledging accomplishments, crafting environments of trust and acceptance, and recognizing the transformative power of vulnerability and boundary-setting.

The pursuit of inner calm is a continual process. It necessitates introspection, tenacity, bravery, and, above all, self-affection. By merging age-old healing rituals with contemporary resources, confronting long-standing apprehensions, and challenging systemic hindrances, Black women can foster an environment conducive to comprehensive well-being. This is a restorative journey where individual healing not only betters oneself but also creates ripples, strengthening the broader community by setting positive examples and fostering mutual support.

Ultimately, to protect one's peace is a profound act of self-acknowledgment. It signifies a dedication to personal value, development, and restoration. It's about taking control of one's story, navigating through life with tenacity, empathy, and affection, and actively engaging in self-reflection and community dialogue to reshape the narrative for the next generation. May this book stand as a lighthouse of optimism, an affirmation of the unwavering spirit of Black women, and a continual resource for all who aspire to discover and safeguard their tranquility.

about the author

Elizabeth Leiba is a writer, college professor, and advocate for Black businesswomen. She has over 100,000 followers on LinkedIn who range in age, race, background, and location primarily in the US, Canada, and the UK.

Her passion for Black history changed her life. It catapulted her into a fulfilling line of work as a powerful advocate of social justice and equity for Black women, especially Black businesswomen. Elizabeth strives to create resources that support, empower, and amplify Black businesswomen and their businesses.

She was featured in the 2020 *New York Times* article "Black LinkedIn Is Thriving. Does LinkedIn Have a Problem With That?" highlighting her social justice advocacy work. The response to this article spurred her to launch her online, accessible e-learning platform, Black History & Culture Academy. This incredible educational resource earned her the recognition of a LinkedIn TOP VOICE in Education in 2020.

She is also the host of *Black Power Moves*, a podcast on EBONY Media Covering Black America Podcast Network, and is a published writer. Her most recent writing includes an op-ed piece on racial profiling for CNN, which had over two million views on their news website.

In early 2022, Elizabeth launched her website directory, Black Women Handle Business, the premier website for Black women entrepreneurs and professionals to network, collaborate, and share resources.

She is the bestselling author of *I'm Not Yelling*, and resides in Washington, DC.

Mango Publishing, established in 2014, publishes an eclectic list of books by diverse authors—both new and established voices—on topics ranging from business, personal growth, women's empowerment, LGBTQ+ studies, health, and spirituality to history, popular culture, time management, decluttering, lifestyle, mental wellness, aging, and sustainable living. We were named 2019 *and* 2020's #1 fastest growing independent publisher by *Publishers Weekly*. Our success is driven by our main goal, which is to publish high-quality books that will entertain readers as well as make a positive difference in their lives.

Our readers are our most important resource; we value your input, suggestions, and ideas. We'd love to hear from you—after all, we are publishing books for you!

Please stay in touch with us and follow us at:

Facebook: Mango Publishing
Twitter: @MangoPublishing
Instagram: @MangoPublishing
LinkedIn: Mango Publishing
Pinterest: Mango Publishing
Newsletter: mangopublishinggroup.com/newsletter

Join us on Mango's journey to reinvent publishing, one book at a time.